In Search of
PRINCESS
WHITE
DEER

In Search of
PRINCESS WHITE DEER

THE BIOGRAPHY OF ESTHER DEER

PATRICIA O. GALPERIN

FLINT &
FEATHER
PRESS

FIRST EDITION

All rights reserved, including the right of
reproduction in whole or in part in any form.

Copyright © 2012 by Patricia O. Galperin

Published by
Flint & Feather Press
42 Alpine Trail
Sparta, NJ 07871

Manufactured in the United States of America

ISBN: 978-0-9897877-0-3
Library of Congress Control Number: 2012906029

0 9 8 7 6 5 4 3 2 1

Cover and interior design by Sheila Hart Design, Inc.
Photo credits appear on page 227 of this book, and constitute an extension of this copyright page

Contents

DEDICATION... 9
PROLOGUE.. 11
CHAPTER ONE: TO THE FAMILY BORN.................... 19
   Heritage 19
   Chief Running Deer 21
   A Career Hazard 25
   Indians Call at City Hall................................ 27
   The Last Stage Call—Pan-American Exposition.......... 27
   The Quiet Life... 30
   The Akwesasne Wolf Belt 30
   Death of Running Deer 33
   James Deer.. 34
   Khartoum—The Nile Expedition to Rescue
      General "Chinese" Gordon 35
   Georgette Osborne Deer 41
   James Meets His Bride 43

CHAPTER TWO: WILD WEST SHOWS...................... 47
   Daniel Boone—Indians of the Past 47
   A Copyrighted Act...................................... 51
   Walter Main 54
   The Great Train Robbery 55
   Queen of the Highway................................. 56
   Texas Jack's Wild West Show—South Africa 58
   Journeys 63
   Dresden, Germany...................................... 65
   Karl May and Rudolf Lebius 67
   The End of the Act—Indians of the Past.............. 70

CHAPTER THREE: A CAREER OF HER OWN 73
  From Russia with Love 73
  A Brief Marriage 74
  Keith—Vaudeville 81
  A Day in the Life on the Keith Circuit 88
  A Family Evening Turned Bad 89
  Peppy De Albrew—Atlantic City 92
  From Wigwam to White Lights 96
  Dancing on the Radio 100
  Ziegfeld Follies 102
  The Second Seattle Revue &
    Erlanger Dillingham Ziegfeld Concert 104
  Dancing on Rooftops: The Midnight Frolic 105
  Ziegfeld Nine O'clock Frolic 1921 107
  Broadway 108
  Hitchy-Koo 1919 108
  Tip Top 114
  Not Without My Permission;
    The Astute Businesswoman 116
  The Yankee Princess 118
  Lucky 120
  Paris 1928 122

CHAPTER FOUR: THE LAKE MOHAWK CONNECTION 127
  Building A Dream 127
  The Fifth Anniversary 133
  The Tenth Anniversary 136

CHAPTER FIVE: ARTISTS AND SCHOLARS................... 141
   The Artists 141
   Arnold Genthe 142
   Cooper Union Woman's Art School.................. 143
   Ulric H. Ellerhusen 144
   Alfred Chaney Johnston 146
   E. O. Hoppé 146
   Alexander Stirling Calder 148
   Paramount Pictures................................. 149
   Curt E. Engelbrecht 149
   Music.. 150
   The Color of Costumes............................. 151
   The Scholars.. 153
   The Nature of Syncopation 155
   PBS 156
   The Smithsonian National Museum
      of the American Indian......................... 156

CHAPTER SIX: LIFE BEYOND THE FOOTLIGHTS 159
   The Personal Side................................... 159
   Romance—Real, Imagined, and Still Talked About 162
   Young Love.. 162
   The Farmer's Son 162
   A Boy from Back Home............................. 164
   The Race Car Driver 165
   The Bandleader..................................... 166
   Native American Activism, Patriotism,
      Civic and Social Activities...................... 168
   1937—A Very Good Year........................... 172
   Russet Mantle 173

Political Blunder and the Iroquois Confederacy........... 174
Indians Bid for Manhattan............................ 178
Feather from an Indian Headdress..................... 179
Pursuit of the Wolf Belt............................. 181
Death Tolls The Death of James Deer.................. 183
The Passing of the Family............................ 186
The Death of Georgette Deer......................... 187
Living to Be One Hundred............................ 190

REFERENCES 193

PHOTO CREDITS 227

Dedication

This book is dedicated to my husband, Allan Galperin, for his love, encouragement, and unquestioning support throughout the writing of it; to my friend, Sylvia Karonhiahawi Goodleaf Trudeau, because the telling of this story would not have been possible without her invaluable assistance and deep family love; and most of all, to the memory of Esther Louise Georgette Deer.

A special acknowledgement to Sue Ellen Herne and the Akwesasne Museum; to Martin Loft and the Kanien'kehaka Raotitiohkwa Cultural Center in Kahnawake; and to Chief Darren Bonaparte and his website, "The Wampum Chronicles." Unknowingly, you were often the voice of reason in my search to understand Native American history and customs.

Prologue

Esther Deer was waiting for a telephone call from the President of the United States. She had been waiting for this day her entire life; no, not the phone call, her one hundredth birthday. She had always wanted to live to be one hundred.

She had risen early, not something she was accustomed to doing, as she preferred to sleep in after staying up late into the night, reading. Time hadn't altered that habit, as she had been doing so since her days in vaudeville and on Broadway, and maybe even earlier, when the whole family had performed in their own border drama at theatres. But time had altered other aspects, including the recent addition of an attendant who helped her dress. Still, she lived on her own, independently. It wasn't that long ago that she scared the neighbor who came rushing into her apartment, because the sounds she heard led her to think Esther was in distress, only to find her doing push-ups off the bathtub. The memory made her laugh. She still exercised when she could.

The president calling her today would certainly be different from the time she had traveled to the White House to hand-deliver an invitation to the president to attend the Grand Council of the Ancient Iroquois Confederacy. That was in 1937.

Esther knew she was the last in a line of three generations of Mohawk entertainers who had worked together; it had started with her grandfather, Chief Running Deer, in the 1860s, and it was ending with her. She was known onstage as Princess White Deer and had become internationally renowned for her Indian acts and dancing.

She had a wonderful career. She led a magical life. She hadn't realized that by wishing to live to be one hundred, just about everyone she ever loved or knew wouldn't be here to celebrate with her. She missed them all. Lately, she thought about them more often. Her dear father and sweet angel mother—Esther had always called her that—were gone; gone for decades. She kept their memories near; she still lived in the same apartment she had shared with her mother at the Monterey, with a second-floor view of Lafayette Square and of the waterfall across the street in Morningside Park.

She was excited that her niece Sylvia and her husband Ray would be arriving shortly from Canada. She loved Sylvia, the daughter of her best friend and cousin, May. They were like sisters. May's children honored her by calling her Auntie, and she called them her nieces and nephew. May too was gone, lost to breast cancer shortly after her mother had passed. She missed her; she had shared everything with May.

She had loved her long stays with May at her house on the reservation in Kahnawake. She seemed to spend half her time there. She had so many wonderful memories of Kahnawake and the dances. Oh, the dances! Dances held in her honor. She hadn't traveled to the reservation much since May's death, preferring to stay with Sylvia across the St. Lawrence River in Lachine. Since turning ninety, she hadn't traveled much at all.

She couldn't wait to show Sylvia the newspaper story, "Princess White Deer Turns 100 Years Old!" Sylvia, her champion, would enjoy it. *The People's Voice* had run the full-page article the day before, on Halloween. It was accompanied by two photographs: one of her at the White House, delivering the invitation to President Roosevelt, and the other of her with Sylvia. That picture was from 1970, when she was 79. Even then she was told she was a beautiful woman. Imagine that! Still, she was delighted to be remembered.

She had time to think and muse before their arrival, and let the memories pour over her.

In a flash of her mind's eye, she saw her grandfather, Running Deer. She remembered seeing him perform for the last time before he retired, at the Pan-American Exposition in Buffalo; that was 1901. Although she was very young, she, too, had performed there, riding in her native dress. There were sad events that occurred at the exposition; President McKinley was assassinated, and Geronimo was displayed in handcuffs on the midway for the world to gawk at. Esther remembered crying when she saw him. She had heard the adults talking about him. What a sad sight for a child to see.

Most of her grandfather's achievements were before her time. Still she remembered them all. Family stories were told and retold; our Mohawk tradition. He was an important man, a hereditary chief and keeper of the Akwesasne Wolf Belt.

Her thoughts shifted as she remembered her first time singing before an audience, in the play *Queen of the Highway*. Her mother had a major role, and her father and uncle were in it too. They called her Little White Deer. She was twelve years old. A newspaper wrote a very complimentary review about her singing. Esther wondered if that could have been her first newspaper review.

Her career began at a young age, performing with her family in a type of play known as a border drama, which was popular with the people at that time as they clamored to be entertained by tales of pioneers, the frontier, Indians, and the West. She grew up while traveling the United States with the whole family, performing in *Daniel Boone, Indians of the Past*. Her father and his brother, John, copyrighted their act as "The Famous Deer Brother Indian Trick Riders of the World."

Later, they all traveled to South Africa with Texas Jack's Wild West Show and performed there along with the Cohan family, whose children, Josephine and George, were close in age to her. George Cohan would later be famous. Will Rogers was there too, just starting out his career. Crossing the Atlantic was exciting, and everything in South Africa was exotic to her, even the meerkats.

Esther's train of thought shifted again; she began thinking about Europe. The Deer family traveled there and performed for the next four years. Sometimes they played two shows in one night, and sometimes four. They met dignitaries and royalty. Esther was always surprised to have such lovely gifts showered upon her; some she still treasured, tucked away with all her mementos in her special room. Later the family joined Colonel Cummins' show and traveled two more years. She spent her teenage years mostly in Europe.

She remembered the thrill and excitement of the unknown when she went solo; she was a young woman of nineteen. She traveled in Eastern Europe, then headed farther east to Russia with her own production of Indian acts. It wasn't long before she attracted the attention of the Tsar's family and gave a command performance.

She was proud of her Mohawk heritage, proud of how it played a part in her success and set her apart from the other actors, dancers, and singers onstage. It always sustained her. The acclaim had been very rich and rewarding, and most importantly, she had made her family proud of her.

It was also there, so far away, that she had fallen in love, like in a fairy tale, with a handsome prince. He was as exotic to her as she was to him. They had married during the blitz in England: Princess White Deer and her Count Krasicki.

How different her life would have been if the war hadn't happened, changing everything; she would have lived her life as the Countess Krasicka. She would never have been onstage in New York City, and her career would have ended in Russia. The war forced her to return to the U. S. She lost Alex in 1916, on the front fighting for Russia. She plunged into work.

Her thoughts jumped back to all the traveling she had done: B. F. Keith's vaudeville circuit, the Liberty Bonds campaign, and entertaining the troops at the camps. She had a headline show of Indian acts, and marquees lit up the street with her name.

Scenes flitted through her mind. She mused over the memories as she glanced across her room at the framed pictures on her bureau; her father as a young man, before he traveled down the Nile to Khartoum to aid the British in the attempted rescue of General "Chinese" Gordon; another of her mother with her long, beautiful hair flowing down to her knees. She was so tiny in stature, with a seventeen-inch waist, and yet so brave at trick riding—jumping back and forth, from horse to horse, in the race for the bride with her father and uncle as part of "The Famous Deer Brothers Trick Riders of the World." There was her own portrait in the beautiful dress she wore when she danced with her partner, Peppy De Albrew, in Atlantic City; and on another shelf was her favorite photo from a day spent relaxing on the beach at Atlantic City with Eddie Cantor and Abe Lyeman. She even started a bare-leg fad! They were wonderful days, though brief.

Her thoughts now leaped ahead to the time she danced in her Indian act with Ziegfeld. Oh, how she remembered the beautiful sets and costumes! *Ziegfeld Follies* was the toast of the town. That led to being noticed by Raymond Hitchcock. She hadn't thought of him in years. She joined his *Hitchy-Koo*

1919 review and sang Cole Porter's "Old Fashion Garden;" it was considered quite a novelty to have two native performers in it. They toured the United States with nineteen boxcars of scenes, props, costumes, actors, and crew. It was a very big production. They didn't travel in that fashion any longer.

Then came the whirlwind years when she had roles in four Broadway plays, performing in the musicals *Hitchy-Koo, Tip Top, The Yankee Princess,* and *Lucky.* Newspapers always highlighted her doings, and although they didn't always get the facts right, it was still good publicity. She received more attention than any other cast member, and often their parts were bigger than hers. The press once called her a "novelty act," and she recalled even being tagged as "bizarre" under a really good photograph.

Leading photographers and famous sculptors all wrote to ask her to pose for them, wanting to work with Princess White Deer. Each turn in her career brought her more acclaim. It was a good career that spanned nearly four decades. It ended on a high note, performing in Paris; but not before she was chosen by the architects of a new community called Lake Mohawk, to dedicate the lake to the Mohawk people. What a thrill that was to have people come out to see her in that town in the northern New Jersey countryside! They even named White Deer Plaza for her.

It wasn't intended, it was never announced; she had just slipped into retirement, easing away from full-time stage commitments when she returned from Paris. She accepted invitations to perform in benefits and Indian events, or limited engagements. She preferred to give these types of performances over Broadway musicals, which were far too rigorous. Esther had become more involved in championing her father's native causes; she assisted him with publicity over the next decade.

It made her smile to think of her father's amazing friendships with King Haakon of Norway, the fighter Jack Dempsey, and the comedian Harry Lauder. She sighed, thinking how few are the names of the past that are remembered today. Back then, they were headliners.

So many years of dancing and singing had taken their toll. For most dancers, it was a short career. She too had her stage injuries, no one was immune. Entertainment was changing. Younger women with boundless energy vied for roles and were moving forward. She was still dancing at forty. No one seemed to realize that she was already thirty years old when she was chosen by the photographer, Hoppé to be one of his beauties. She had always kept herself fit and trim.

It was entertainment that had changed. The theatres and halls had closed as film became all the rage. The novelty of silent movies gave way to "talkies," and Hollywood beckoned to hopeful stars. Vaudeville was fading from favor, as movie palaces were becoming the new public amusement. She had leaped from border dramas and Wild West shows to vaudeville, headlined with the best on B. F. Keith's circuit, and crossed over to the new fashion of entertainment on Broadway with Ziegfeld's reviews, and then on to four Broadway musicals. She had done it all.

She wouldn't say she had retreated from the stage; it was more like she had dissolved in the mist when she left the stage and entered private life. She had traveled the world working for nearly four decades. She hadn't wanted to travel more. Traveling had run its course.

She had colleagues whom she liked, but she didn't have close personal friends in the business. There was no one she was particularly close with. She preferred the company and love of her family. She hadn't kept in touch with the theatre world.

She had always been a very private person. She didn't talk about her lost love or any personal sorrow. She shared happiness, mostly. She didn't keep a journal. Neither did she keep much in the way of personal mementoes: no theatre stubs, birthday cards, or correspondence. She hadn't given interviews. She accepted invitations and was always happy to attend. She enjoyed the company of others, but she didn't invite anyone to New York or to her apartment, other than family.

She was pleased that she could say it had been an enchanting and wonderful life and that she had enjoyed every moment. A very satisfying life it was.

After thinking about this, Esther knew that all she was going to leave to posterity was her public image. Sylvia, her champion, would see to it. Soon, she knew, she would be joining her family with the Great Spirit, but not today. Today President George Bush would call her, her niece would come to visit, and she would attend a small reception that had been arranged in her honor, for she was one hundred years old.

CHAPTER ONE
To the Family Born

Sometimes, the telling of a life story doesn't begin with the person's birth. To look back on a life one must look even further, to the ancestors, and travel the course of their lives. For we not only inherit our genes, our nationality, and our family traditions, but often we inherit our own life's calling. All of these are conditions that lead up to the beginning of a life, when the story of that life is yet to unfold.

The telephone, automobile, record player, and airplane were yet to be invented. The skyscrapers of New York City had yet to be built. Travel was by steam ship—to cross the Atlantic—or by train—to cross the continent. People traveled by horse, with cart or sleigh attached, on dirt roads. Paved highways that connected the country were yet to be envisioned. It was during this time that Esther Deer, Princess White Deer, would be born into an ancient people with a rich, deep culture. Ken Tio Kwi Osta would be born a Mohawk.

HERITAGE

In ancient times, the nations of the northeast part of North America (Mohawk, Oneida, Seneca, Cayuga, Onondaga, and Tuscarora) formed a confederacy and created a governing system that is known as the Great Law of Peace. It is one of the few examples in the world where nations have come together for the purpose of peace. This confederacy is also known as the Haudenosaunee Confederacy, or Six Nation Confederacy. Haudenosaunee means "people who build" or "people of the longhouse."

The basis of Mohawk beliefs, their values, traditions, and philosophies are formed by their creation story, the Two Row Wampum Treaty, the Confederacy of the Iroquois, and the "seventh generation" concept that shapes their unique view of the world.

The Mohawk Nation is sovereign. It consists of the Kahnawake, whose community lies just across the St. Lawrence River, south of Montreal; Kanehsatàke, on the Ottawa River; Akwesasne, south of Cornwall and in New York State, east of Massena; Tyendinaga at Deseronto, east of Belleville and Gibson, southeast of Georgian Bay near Bala; and Ganienkeh, north of Plattsburgh, New York.

The People of the Longhouse are the original government of the Kanienkehaka (Mohawk). Their jurisdiction comes from the Great Law of Peace. The Kanienkehaka has three clans or extended families: they are the Bear, the Turtle, and the Wolf. It is a matrilineal society; the women pass on the clan through their children (much the same as Judaism).

They discovered the value of working together in a peaceful and respectful manner, in a democratic frame of governance provided by the Great Law. Belief in the creation story of their beginnings and duties as human beings, the instruction of the Two Row Wampum on how to interrelate with other governments and nations, and the concept of the "seventh generation" that teaches respect for their descendants have all combined to sustain the Mohawk Nation.

In the latter half of the nineteenth century, Akwesasne and other Mohawk communities experienced a cultural renaissance. A cottage industry was born that still thrives today, of black ash splint and sweet grass baskets, beadwork, and cradleboards. Non-native interest grew in part out of the excitement of the Wild West shows that captured their imaginations and the lacrosse (Tewaarathon) exhibition held during the Royal Visit to Canada.

Both of these events launched Mohawk into careers of trick riders and circus performers in well-paying Wild West shows that toured the world, as well as careers as lacrosse players who joined leagues. Mohawks adapted their ways to a new world without losing their identity in a society that was assimilating the cultural values of other native communities.

It was also the time of the Industrial Revolution and the emergence of the steel industry. Kahnawake Mohawk men were at the center of it all. Originally hired on as laborers, they soon were scaling iron beams to inspect the work. Construction companies recognized their fearlessness of heights and considered them natural born steel workers. Soon these companies trained them for more dangerous jobs as riveters and connector gangs. Mohawk ironworkers spread out across the United States and Canada, working on major landmarks we know today. A few of the structures Mohawk men have built include the Empire State Building, the World Trade Center, Sears Tower, the CN Tower, and the Golden Gate Bridge.

CHIEF RUNNING DEER

Long before Esther Deer was born, her grandfather was already achieving great success. Chief Running Deer was known as the last hereditary chief of the Mohawk tribe. He was the last to hold the Alliance of the Wampum belt for the Six Nations.

In his younger days, Running Deer was famous for his skill in the one-mile run. He had participated in the games held for the Royal Visit to Canada in 1860 and was presented with a medal from the Prince of Wales, who later became King Edward VII of England. The medal was one of Running Deer's most prized possessions during his life.

All this had happened before his career in Wild West shows. It was a time when boys became men at a much earlier age than they do now.

Chief Running Deer—a.k.a. Ta Si Ta Leri, and also known as John Deer—was born in either 1834 or 1839 on the St. Regis Reservation in Canada. Both his parents were descendants of important hereditary chiefs. His wife, Esther Loft, was a distant relation of Joseph Brant, the famous Loyalist Indian, one of the most well known Native Americans of his generation. Two of Esther's sisters married into the family. Her second-oldest sister married Isaac Brant, Joseph's first son, and her eldest sister married his other son, Seth Brant.

Esther Loft and Running Deer had five children: John, Mary (Williams), James, Lydia, and George. The children were raised in the family enterprise as theatrical performers and rough riders.

Running Deer was one of the first Indians to give exhibi-

The Family of Chief Running Deer, c. late 1880s. Left to Right: James Deer, John Deer, Chief John Running Deer, Esther Loft Deer, Lydia Deer, Mary Deer. Center: George Deer.

tions to the public. In the early 1860s, he had an all-Indian troupe that performed in the William Washburn shows.

Rarely were any of the Indian performers given credit as actors. Neither did it seem to matter to them if they were billed as Apache, Sioux, or Shawnee Indians. They performed the roles assigned, Indian, Cowboy, or Mexican; it didn't matter because they were working and providing for their families. For them it was a better opportunity than the few choices left for them on the reservations.

During the 1880s Chief Running Deer rose up from this obscurity, and his name was prominently displayed on handbills and in advertisements, although his tribe was the whim of the proprietors.

He appeared on the rosters of the Kickapoo Indian Medicine Company and the Umatilla Medicine Show in several of their touring companies over the decade.

Medicine shows, a product of patent medicine companies, would hire performers and pitchmen to sell their wares, usually in areas neighboring the company; but they covered an area as wide as the United States and Canada. Often the medicine show was the only form of entertainment that came to a town or village, and it was met with great fanfare. Towns celebrated its arrival by closing stores and schools. People dressed up in their finest attire for the event.

The agenda of the medicine show was simple: offer a free show, which gathered the crowd. Entertain them with acts such as singers, comic sketches, jugglers, acrobats, music (banjo was the most common), magic, ventriloquism, and dancing. Somewhere during the performance, when they had the crowd's attention, the pitchman was brought out. He was often called "Professor" or "Doctor." He would then pitch the medicine of the company he represented. Some shows adopted Indian names and some named their medicine for Indian remedies.

The "Under the White Tents" column of The New York Clipper reported that the Umatilla Medicine Company No. 7 was currently touring central Illinois and doing well despite the rains, and listed Chief Running Deer among its roster in July of 1891.

In 1892, Chief Running Deer performed in Hayesville, Ohio at the Old Opera House with the Indian Medicine Company, and sold Umatilla Tonic. His name, along with many other performers who came through town, is written on the dressing room walls there. It was a tradition for acting companies, medicine shows, "enlightened lecturers," musicians, and traveling troupes to sign and leave the dates of their performance, which go back to its opening in 1886. Today the Old Opera House has been restored to its original condition and is listed on the National Register of Historic Buildings.

Chief Running Deer had performed with leading Wild West shows of the times, traveling around the United States. From renowned shows such as P. T. Barnum, 101 Ranch, Stowe Brothers, Tompkin's Wild West Shows, John Robinson's Circus, Davis & Keogh, Peck and Fursman, and Texas Jack's Wild West Shows, to minor regional touring companies such as McGolfin's Wild West, Winan's Medicine Company, and the St. Regis Indian Show, Chief Running Deer and his Indian troupe played them all.

Robinson's advertised its week's engagement commencing February 16, 1891, in *The Illustrated Buffalo Express,* headlining "An Encampment of Genuine Sioux and Blackfeet Indians direct from Pine Ridge Agency. Celebrated Chief Running Deer and his Band of Noted Warriors! The Great Ghost Dance. Ten Cents General Admission; Five, Ten, and Fifteen cents extra for reserved seats." Running Deer and his sons, with their trained bear and dog, had worked for Robinson's earlier in February, 1888, at the Dime Museum.

In 1894, while traveling to Lawrence, Kansas with the St. Regis Indian Show Company, he was photographed by

W. S. Tanner, a picture preserved by the Library of Congress; he was also shot with family members. He appeared in the Thomas Edison film that was a first in show-business history, an early movie that became an important milestone in picture making, *The Great Train Robbery*. This was a familiar role for Running Deer, as he played it in the Davis & Keogh play production of *The Great Train Robbery* by Scott Marble that toured the Midwestern states in 1896 and 1897.

Gordon Lillie, also known as "Pawnee Bill," once wrote that Chief Running Deer was one of the greatest acts he had ever seen in his life.

The Pawnee Bill Shows originated in Montreal, about ten miles outside of Caughnawaga (present day Kahnawake), and he hired Mohawk entertainers from there to be part of his troupe. When Pawnee Bill merged his shows with Buffalo Bill in 1908, the Caughnawaga entertainers were dropped as Buffalo Bill acquired his native talent through the offices of the Bureau of Indian Affairs. Any record of a Caughnawaga performer on the Buffalo Bill payroll is nonexistent.

A CAREER HAZARD

Being a Wild West show performer could sometimes be hazardous and bring about run-ins with the law. From parade-sideline squabbles to genuine knife fights on the stage, the Deer men were not immune.

In 1890, in Birmingham, Alabama, Chief Running Deer was performing with the Stowes' Wild West Show. The story was reported in detail in the *Age Herald* weekly newspaper. It was typical for the time that the performing show would parade through town to draw spectators to come out and see the performance. As the procession went up Twenty-second Street, crowds of children, who behaved more like urchins, followed them on either side. Little boys stood on the sidelines with eyes wide from reading terrifying Wild West tales, and watched the descriptions come to life.

Chief Running Deer, mounted on his horse, sat tall and dignified in the saddle. His clothing was described in great detail. He wore "a wampum belt from which was suspended two long barreled pistols and a glittering ugly looking bowie knife girth about his loins, while in his right hand he carried a tomahawk," to the delight of children. He wore "a breast plate of tin, which resembled an inverted coffee pot cover." His face looked even more ferocious with its dabs of red paint, and feathers stood atop his hatless head, but the children eyed him with envy and admiration.

As the parade was nearing Second Avenue, two little boys picked up a few pebbles and threw them at the horse. Chief Running Deer saw them do it! He didn't approve of mistreating an animal. He gave a loud whoop and chased after them with his tomahawk raised menacingly in the air. The boys took flight down Second Avenue with Chief Running Deer galloping behind them. They ran for safety into a store, but Chief Running Deer did not stop galloping in pursuit until he was on the very sidewalk in front. Just then, Officer Gardner sprang forward and grabbed the horse by the reins. Running Deer still had his tomahawk held high, and Officer Gardner pulled out his pistol and aimed it at the Chief, who was still indignant over the horse's ill treatment by the children.

The situation could have turned into a tragedy had not one of the Stowe brothers stepped forward and intervened, quieting the upset Running Deer. A police van was sent for, but the Chief kept exclaiming he was not guilty. He refused to get in, so Mr. Stowe entered the van first, Chief Running Deer followed; and together they went off to the city prison where they were met by the Chief of Police.

The crowd that had followed the van had grown so large that

the office doors had to be closed to keep them out. Two charges were made against Chief Running Deer by Officer Gardner: one of reckless riding, the other of resisting an officer. Mr. Stowe entered a fifty dollar bond for each charge. Upon leaving, Chief Running Deer shook hands with the Chief Pickard. The two little boys who started the ruckus were not arrested.

INDIANS CALL AT CITY HALL
Chief Running Deer performed in many different venues. *The New York Times* reported in 1896 that "Indians Call at City Hall." Chief Running Deer, along with Split Bark, Crow Foot, American Horse, Long Feather, and Red Deer, all in full costume with feathers and war paint, called on Mayor Strong to pay their respects. The mayor was at a board meeting so his secretary, Job Hedges, did the honors instead. They were there as members of the theatrical troupe to promote the romantic opera, *Brian Boru*, which opened on October 19 at the Broadway Theatre. *Brian Boru* went on to play the Columbus Theatre in February 1897 and the People's Theatre in September of that same year.

THE LAST STAGE CALL—PAN-AMERICAN EXPOSITION
Running Deer's last stage appearance was in 1901 at the Pan-American Exposition held in Buffalo, New York. About five million people visited the exposition between May and November. Electricity was a new invention, unfamiliar to many people who were accustomed to gaslight. The exposition came alive with 160,000 electric lights every evening, giving Buffalo the nickname of "City of Light."

The Six Nation's Iroquois stockade exhibit, funded by the government, was located near the Forestry Building; whereas the Indian Congress of 42 Tribes, described in the official catalog as "700 Indians representing 42 distinct tribes and living in their aboriginal and primitive state"—which had the big draw of Apache Chief Geronimo, who was officially in Federal custody—was located at the last building on the Midway heading south, on the opposite side of the exposition grounds.

Chief Running Deer's son James was a daredevil bareback rider with the Indian Congress. During one of the performances he lost his hold and was thrown, only narrowly escaping death. The horse stepped on his right hand, and his head was cut. His injuries were attended to at the Pan-American Expo infirmary.

C. O. Arnold, the official photographer for the Pan-American Exposition, captured their exhibit for posterity, and perhaps could not resist the image of Indian children in costume: a little Mohawk girl named White Deer standing with Hoek See Ocka, a Winnebago boy.

President William McKinley was not present at the opening ceremonies due to his wife's illness, and Vice President Theodore Roosevelt did the honors. With hopes of boosting sagging attendance at the end of summer, the organizers rescheduled President McKinley's visit for September 6.

On that fateful day, after a visit to Niagara Falls, the President was to attend a public reception at the exhibition's Temple of Music that was to last ten minutes. A young man with a handkerchief over his right hand made his way along the receiving line. When President McKinley extended his hand, the man shot him twice. The crowd wrestled him to the ground before a third shot could be fired. Leon Czolgosz was taken into police custody.

President McKinley was in good condition but was operated on at the exposition hospital because doctors had feared that moving him would be too risky. The doctors were unable to remove one of the two bullets, but believed that it was lodged in fatty tissue and wouldn't pose a threat. For several days his conditioned improved. He was moved to the home of John Milburn, president of the exposition, to continue recuperating. But on Friday, September 13, he took a turn for the worse. Vice President Theodore Roosevelt was sent for, but before he could reach Buffalo, President McKinley died on Saturday, September 14, 1901. An hour later. in the presence of about fifty people, Roosevelt was sworn in by United States District Judge John R. Hazel as the twenty-sixth President of the United States.

Deer's Indian Village—Redmen Welcome—Pan-American Exposition, 1901. John Deer on left, lassoing cowboy; James and Georgette Deer at ticket booth; Princess White Deer on white horse, center; Chief Running Deer, center right.

The remainder of the Pan-American Exposition was somber as it had become the location of the nation's tragedy. What should have been Buffalo's finest hour turned into the city's darkest.

THE QUIET LIFE

Chief Running Deer recreated himself and as the proprietor of the Old International Hotel in Malone, New York...a business he had purchased in 1887, near the boundary of the St. Regis Reservation. The hotel was built in 1780.

Yet you could hardly consider his a quiet or retiring life. Excitement rivaling Wild West shows could be found right at home.

The Ogdensburg Advance and *The Palladium* both reported a shootout—called "Quite a shooting affair"—that took place at the St. Regis on a particular Saturday night, July 30, 1897.

James Carpenter of Cornwall, a baker in the village, and Lewis Terence (or Terants) both spent Saturday night at the hotel. During the night Mr. Terence tried to reenter after hours and was asked to leave by the proprietor. Instead, he attempted to gain access through an open first-floor window in the rear of the building at the same moment Carpenter, the occupant of the room, had gotten up to close it. The two men began having a verbal altercation when the proprietor, Mr. Running Deer, hearing the heated voices, entered the room and, thinking that both men were trying to enter, fired at them.

The bullet entered Mr. Carpenter's elbow and exited his wrist, grazing the cheek of Mr. Terence and slicing through his ear. Dr. McConnell was called and dressed their wounds. Both men recovered.

THE AKWESASNE WOLF BELT

The Akwesasne Wolf Belt was last in the possession of Chief Running Deer. The legend behind the Wolf Belt had been passed down orally from generation to generation.

The belt represents the treaty between the British King, George III, and the head Chief of the Praying Indians (Caughnawaga, St. Regis, Oka, and their allies) with two figures clasping hands in friendship in the center of the belt. On each end, seven purple rows of shell wampum beads represent the Seven Nations, the union of Iroquois and Algonquin settlements encouraged by the French Catholic priests who had influenced and converted them to Christianity.

These settlements consisted of the Mohawk, Algonquin, and Nipissing bands at Lake of Two Mountains; part of the Caughnawaga band; the Oswegatchie band, which was near Ogdensburg, New York; the Huron of Lorett; and the Abenakis of St. Francis.

The white band between the seven purple rows means a path of peace. The east and west end is guarded by the Wolf Clan, symbolized by purple, full-bodied wolf figures facing outward, watchful of danger. The hereditary keeper of the Eastern Door of the Longhouse was of the Wolf Clan and the Mohawk people; and the Western Door keeper was also of the Wolf Clan but of the Seneca people. The Mohawks were never in the alliance with France; they only traded with them.

When the Mohawks formed their community, belts of wampum were created to represent the codes that the people lived by regarding residence, membership, and territorial boundaries. The Akwesasne Wolf Belt was accepted by the Mohawk people around 1747 and was recognized and acknowledged by the Great Law, the original constitution. The Great Law was given to the People of the Longhouse centuries ago and unified warring nations into a peaceful alliance, which was the first "United Nations" and laid the foundation for the constitution of the United States and the Charter of the United Nations. The belt was made of Quahog clamshell on a simple loom and is 14 rows wide and approximately 184 beads long. The emblem represents the pledge: "We will live together or die together. We promise this as long as the water runs, the skies do shine and the night brings rest." (Henry Carrington, 11th United States Census Extra Census Bulletin on the Six Nations of New York, 1892. p. 76.) Today, it is the insignia on the letterhead of the Mohawk Council of Akwesasne.

The historian and author Darren Bonaparte believes that "the Akwesasne Wolf Belt served a dual purpose: it is both a recognition of our claim to the territory on which we live and an acceptance of the Mohawks of Akwesasne into the 'silver covenant chain' with the British."

A few years after the *United States Census Extra Census Bulletin on the Six Nations of New York* and before it was turned over the New York State Museum, a collector acquired the belt from Chief Running Deer. The actual circumstances surrounding the questionable transaction of this priceless piece of heritage are not fully known, other than the fact that the Chief claimed to have lent the belt to a Mrs. Harriet Converse on July 24, 1898. The situation was politically charged, with a lawsuit involving chiefs, regents, and governments.

Correspondence in the 1970s between The University of the State of New York, The State Education Department, and Esther Deer would confirm that it was Mrs. Converse, a non-native folklorist and champion of the Iroquois, who had provided the State of New York with the belt.

Harriet Converse was one of the most active collectors of wampum, which she acquired by both gift and purchase, and was responsible for delivering to the State of New York sixteen wampum belts. One of the most notable women of her day, she was adopted by the Seneca, and the Six Nations made her an honorary chieftainess.

The law that allowed the State Museum to keep the wampum belts would be known as Section 27 of the New York

State Indian Law, which pertains to the custody of the wampum which was originally enacted as Chapter 153, Laws of 1899.

This law directly relates to a lawsuit in 1898 in which the Chiefs of Onondaga were trying to recover four belts that were in the hands of a private collector. Mrs. Converse had persuaded the Onondaga Nation to appoint her their attorney against that collector. It was her letter to him that set the lawsuit in motion. In what would be known as *Onondagas vs. Thatcher*, on October 10, 1897, the Onondaga Nation sued John Boyd Thatcher.

The fact remains that the Wolf Belt has been separated from its people for more than over one hundred years, a very dark chapter in its history. The Wolf Belt was not returned to the Haudenosaunee Confederacy at the Onondaga longhouse on July 6, 1996, by the National Museum of the American Indian and was not witnessed by the Mohawk Nation Council of Chiefs, as has been reported; it is still with the New York State Museum.

DEATH OF RUNNING DEER

On February 12, 1924, Chief Running Deer died at the home of his daughter, Mary Williams, in Caughnawaga, Canada. The cause was pneumonia. No less than five newspapers in northern New York ran his obituary with text reading, "Famous Indian Dies in Quebec," "Old Circus Star," "had many distinctions," "had circus troupe for years," and "conducted hotel on boundary line in St. Regis."

One admiring reporter eulogized in his column: "I was of course enthralled by his tales and certainly somewhat apprehensive about some of them because of their color and also because I had only his word. However, it wasn't long after our meeting that the entire life of this very outstanding man was authenticated. His stories and adventures will live on but, of course, he himself could not for much longer."

Chief Running Deer had lived to see his children marry, his sons continue in the entertainment business, and to see his granddaughter Esther's career soar in three of her four Broadway plays—two starring roles in Ziegfeld's *Frolics* and a solo on the "two-a-day" Keith Circuit. He was aware of her reputation as one of the world's most beautiful women, and at the age of thirty-one she was plucky enough to stop the press. Surely this pleased the showman in him.

Sadly, he had outlived his youngest two children and his wife. His daughter Lydia died before the end of the nineteenth century. His son George died two months shy of his twenty-ninth birthday in Hamburg, Germany on April 7, 1913, from injuries he suffered in a riding accident with a circus. He was buried in the beautiful and renowned Ohlsdorfer Cemetery in Hamburg. Chief Running Deer's wife, Esther Loft, died shortly before him in 1922 at the age of ninety.

A. M. Klein's poem, "Indian Reservation: Caughnawaga," immortalizes him in these lines:

> Where are the tribes, the feathered bestiaries?–
> Rank Aesop's animals erect and red.
> With fur on their names to make all live things kin!–
> Chief Running Deer, Black Bear, Old Buffalo Head?

JAMES DEER

James Deer, also known as Chief Ar Ha Ken Kia Ka or "Cutting the Forest," was the son of Chief Running Deer. Like his father and his father's grandfather, he too would be known as Running Deer in certain circles. He was born on January 3, 1866 in Mexico, New York, and given the name Ar Ha Ken Kia Ka at a time when his father, Running Deer was overseeing a work crew of Indian men tasked with clearing a forest for a white employer. His mother, Esther Loft, was among the women

James Deer, c. late 1880.

accompanying their families on this job. In accordance with Mohawk custom he was named for the task. As the son of a performer, raised in the family business of fearless feats and a zest for excitement, he started out young on his own quest for personal adventure and making his mark upon the world.

KHARTOUM—THE NILE EXPEDITION TO RESCUE GENERAL "CHINESE" GORDON

Before the Aswan Dam was built, the Nile River in Egypt had a series of five cataracts, each of which contained small falls and rapids. The 1880s were a time when the Suez Canal was still new; the British were governing the politically unstable Egypt as a protectorate and, having a huge investment in the canal, were interested in preserving their trade route.

A group of Sudanese insurgents known as the Mahdis, or Mahdists, after their leader Muhammad Ahmad al-Mahdi, were seeking independence as an Islamic Republic in the province of Sudan.

General Charles Gordon, who had earned the moniker "Chinese," had played an important role in suppressing the Taiping uprising, which had threatened European trading in Shanghai. He later held the position of governor of the province of Equatoria in the Sudan, where he mapped the upper Nile and established stations as far south as Uganda. His repression of the slave trade earned him a promotion to Governor-General, but bad health forced him to resign and return to England.

In 1884 he was dispatched by the British Government to Khartoum, the capital of the Sudanese province, to withdraw forces stationed at the Egyptian Garrison and return to Britain. General Gordon ignored the order and soon found himself defending the garrison under siege, trapped within as Mahdi forces stormed the city.

The British Empire sent the well-seasoned commander Lord Wolseley to rescue General Gordon. Wolseley had proven himself in the Red River expedition of 1870; he appreciated the skill of the boatmen on that waterway. The first action he took was to ask the Governor-General of Canada, Lord Lansdowne, to enlist the ranks of "300 good voyageurs from Caughnawaga, St. Regis, and Manitoba as steersmen in boats for the Nile Expedition."

In the fourteen years since Red River, those expert boatmen had moved on, mainly to employment by the railway. But many still maintained their skills. Wolseley set up a central office and had Lt. Col. Frederick Charles Denison oversee recruitment in three regions: Ottawa, Three Rivers, and Caughnawaga. By

August, advertisements were placed, with the terms of service being a six-month contract that also included rations and clothing. The pay for boatmen was 40 dollars a month, and for foremen, 75. A total of 367 men were recruited; of these 86 were Indians from Quebec, Ontario, and Manitoba—and of these men 56 were Caughnawaga Mohawks. Of those 56, two were brothers who had enlisted together; they were James D. Deer and his brother, John Deer, sons of Chief Running Deer.

James later wrote:

> I will never forget my first experience in shooting the Lachine Rapids on a single-layer raft. After the pilot gave the signal to run for the rope to safety which ran the length of the raft, secured tightly, the men ran in haste to the rope to cling as the heavy river was on top of the raft until it reached the foot of the rapids. Well, to our surprise our raft dove into a large hole and we were under water with a strong hold on the rope so as not to get washed away with the rapids.
>
> We lost our hats, and struck rocks that broke up our raft into three parts. The front part broke into two, each corner torn away from the main body with the men clinging to one portion and the other part with two men. The other frontman was farther in the middle and remained with the rest of us. It was a terrible sight after the raft floated on top again. At the bottom of the rapids, there were men in place in boats who helped get the other two pieces of the raft fastened to the main body, and the five men that clung to it were saved. From there on, we traveled along a swift stream with no more rapids with only obstacle being the steering clear of the abutments of the Victoria Bridge at Montreal. The rafts ended up in an eddy at lower Montreal.

Lord Wolseley had visited America in that northern part of Canada where he found out that Indians at that time were the most expert in navigating in dangerous waters. Up to that time there was no white man who ever had the honor of piloting the steamers and the rafts down the Lachine Rapids but the Iroquois Indians.

Further north on the Matawan River and the Ottawa River so much logging was done by large companies where many of the Iroquois Indians were employed, often breaking up the ice early in the spring to make the drive of the logs down the different rapids until they get to a bay of more still waters, where the logs are corralled by a large log boom and then made into rafts in order to keep the logs together to shoot the deep water channels of the rapids.

Some of these rafts were single layer and some double layer which are the best for shooting the rapids like the Lachine. After they are made into large river rafts they are then piloted down the stream and tied up at Caughnawaga harbor where the regular pilots and crew of 12 men to every raft handle the large timber. Two men took each corner with six men in the front and six in the back. The pilot stands up high in the middle of the raft and gives orders to the men in what direction to pull for to get in the right channel to shoot the rapids.

On September 13, 1884, the voyage across the Atlantic began from Montreal aboard the *S.S. Ocean King*, which the War Department had chartered. It met with the death and burial of a Saulteaux Indian, and arrived at Alexandria on October 7 with 800 open, double-ended whalers that were to be taken to Assiout (Assuit) by rail and then on to Assuan (Aswan) as the cargo in Nile barges. The whalers would be put in the water below the First Cataract and taken by Egyptian boatmen to Wadi Halfa to be towed by river steamers. Denison and the expedition crew disembarked at Wadi Halfa on October 26.

Although the expedition was halfway to its destination, the journey from Wadi Halfa to Khartoum was to take three months, covering four cataracts and rapids. The first leg of river journey was to get the empty boats to the head of the Second Cataract. Crews consisting of seven men made two trips, taking the empty boats to Bab el Kebir and walking back three miles to get the next group of boats. It took 10 days to complete this task. As described in *A Sketch Account of Aboriginal Peoples in the Canadian Military*, "On October 31, fifty-six boats were taken up by a combination of towing, rowing and sailing, each crew making three trips and each trip involving the walk back, through clinging sand and under a burning sun."

Most of the voyageurs worked with the infantry and their whalers. A small group of 35 men of Caughnawaga set out under Colonel James Alleyne to reconnoiter further on. They continued to Semneh, considered the most dangerous of the cataracts. A fixed station system was used. Instead of a gang of boatmen accompanying a unit up the river and then returning to repeat the process, Canadians established fixed camps at the wildest points of the river, taking boats through as they came, as they were fully familiar with specific rapids as well as their tidal changes.

The Fourth Cataract was reached in six months, and volunteers were asked to re-engage for another six months at an increased salary of 60 dollars a month. With logging work waiting at home for many and the unbearably hot Sudanese climate, only six foremen and 83 boatmen signed on for the next stretch, with only six Indians among them.

On January 24, 1885, a small infantry detachment reached Khartoum and found that the city had been taken by the

Mahdists and General Gordon was dead. Wolseley's expedition was two days too late.

A retreat was ordered on February 24. The remaining 70 voyageurs had more than 200 boats to run through difficult rapids. As many as seven trips were made in one day. By March the boats reached Korti, and in another few days Denison and his men left for Cairo and Canada. Denison was hospitalized for typhoid fever on arrival in Cairo, but did recover and was awarded the CMG for his service in Egypt.

Lieutenant-Colonel Coleridge Grove, commander at Gemai, wrote "The employment of the voyageurs was a most pronounced success. Without them it is to be doubted whether the boats would have got up at all, and it may be taken as certain that if they had, they would have been far longer in doing so, and the loss of life would have been much greater than has been the case..." Brigadier-General F. W. Grenfell, commander of Nile communication, endorsed Grove's view by stating, "I am of opinion that the Indians were best adapted to working the many rapids. Their skill in handling a boat in water was most marked. The expedition could hardly have done without their valuable aid."

The Egypt Medal (1884–1885) was awarded to 392 Canadian voyageurs with The Nile 1884–85 bar. Of these men, 46 received the Kirbekan bar for actually having reached Khartoum. The Nile 1884–85 bar was awarded to the men serving South of Assuan before March 1885 as part of the expedition to rescue General Gordon. The Kirbekan bar was awarded to the men who actually reached Khartoum and was only awarded along with The Nile 1884–85 bar. Canadians who received this bar were under the command of Lord Wolseley. James Deer and his brother John received the Egypt Medal along with the Kirbekan and Nile bars.

The medal itself is a veiled profile of Queen Victoria facing left. The reverse side is a sphinx on a pedestal with the word "Egypt" above it. The medal is hung from a ribbon of five stripes of alternating blue and white ending in blue, mounted on a straight suspender. The recipient's name is impressed on the rim in sloping capitals.

The brothers also received the Egyptian Bronze Star, awarded by the Khedive in the shape of a five-pointed star, one inch in diameter and connected by a small star and crescent to a laureate bar to which a dark blue ribbon is attached. The front view of the medal is of the Sphinx with desert and pyramids at the rear, inside a double band. Above is imprinted "Egypt 1884," and below, in Arabic, is written "Khedive of Egypt 1301." On the reverse side is monogrammed T. M., for Tewfik Mohamed, surmounted by a crown with crescent and star.

Those who did not return to Canada numbered 16. Six had drowned in the Nile River Cataracts, two had fallen from a rail in Egypt, and eight had died of natural causes. Of the casualties, two men were from Caughnawaga.

The compensation paid to the widows and families of these boatmen was considered very generous for the times. The remainder of the pay the men would have received had they lived out their contract was paid to the families, and special additional grants were paid to those who supported a mother or wife.

After James returned to Caughnawaga, the Montreal publisher J. Lovell printed his experience in a small book entitled *The Canadian Voyageurs in Egypt*. The captain of the contingent, Louis Jackson, also wrote a narrative of his experiences and published *Our Caughnawagas in Egypt* with the Montreal publisher William Drysdale & Co. James chose to travel with Walbach's Show and gave lectures of his adventures on the cataracts on the journey to Khartoum.

GEORGETTE OSBORNE DEER

Georgette Osborne was a child actress who debuted at the age of nine as the character Topsy in *Uncle Tom's Cabin*. From ages nine to thirteen she performed with Fred R. Wren's Dramatic Company. She was his protégé and played many other parts as well, including Eva, Mrs. St. Clair, Aunt Chloe, Emmeline, and Eliza. She graduated from child actress to a beautiful and talented teenage leading lady.

Georgette was born on July 13, 1871, in London, England, to Sir William Hudson Osborne and Lady Mary Osborne, who lived in the suburban charter of London known as Maida Vale near Kilburn Wells, in a Victorian villa of the Grecian style.

Mary Mathewson Holmes Osborne was born on January 17, 1840, to Phoebe Mead Cooley Martin Mathewson (1746–1850), who had eight children by her first husband and four by her second, Mary's father, Gordon Mathewson. Mary in turn had three children with her first husband, Wheeler C. Holmes, and three with William H. Osborne, Georgette's father.

Mary was born on her father's estate in Natchez, Mississippi, and was known onstage as "Birdie Balfore," most likely in theaters around Maida Vale as it had a number of music halls and theaters—and today is the home of the BBC and the recording studio Abbey Road. Theater was in the family blood.

Georgette performed with other Uncle Tom Companies (U.T.C.). She played with Abbey's Uncle Tom's Cabin Company in 1885, again starring as Topsy, a role she would continue to play for the next couple of years, with A.Y. Drapers U.T.C. in 1886 and Peck & Fursman in 1887.

Harriett Beecher Stowe's novel *Uncle Tom's Cabin* was dramatized for seventy-five years, from several months after its publication in 1853, to 1928; it was the most frequently performed of all plays in America. Over its thousands of performances, production companies made changes, adding songs, banjo players, and all-black choirs like the South Carolina Jubilee Singers, as well as stockyard animals and a donkey. The cast was as large as 31 characters, with 18 male roles and

13 female roles. More often than not an actor or actress played two or more roles during the performance. Some made lifelong careers playing one character.

George C. Howard and his wife, Caroline Fox Howard, known as Mrs. G. C. Howard onstage, were such a career story. For thirty-five years he played the part of St. Clare and she took on the role of Topsy, a role she originally obtained by default, as the chosen actress refused to perform in blackface and quit. It was a role Mrs. Howard would play more than five thousand times to rave reviews.

The audiences of the 1880s were connoisseurs of popular plays and especially *Uncle Tom's Cabin*. Popular plays drew from English, French, and American literature. There were dramatizations of Dickens' *Cricket on Earth*, *Chimney Corner*, and *Oliver Twist*; Tennyson's *Dora*; Scott's *The Bride of Lammermoor*, *Rob Roy*, and *The Lady of the Lake*; the French novels *Camille*, *Fanchion the Cricket*, and *Les Misérables*; Germany's *Ingo Mar*; and American author Washington Irving's *Rip Van Winkle*. All were well known to the audience and with a dedicated following. Social problem plays were the most numerous and conspicuous, with titles like *Under the Gaslight*, *The Drunkard*, and *Ten Nights in a Bar Room*.

Georgette Osborne played the lead in *She, Queen of the Highway*, *The Two Orphans*, *Under the Gaslight*, *Rip Van Winkle*, *Fanchion the Cricket*, *Ten Nights in a Bar Room*, *Distrust*, *East Lynn*, *The Austrian*, *The Danitre*, and *The Scout*.

JAMES MEETS HIS BRIDE

In 1888, Georgette Osborne had the opportunity to play her first adult role at the age of sixteen in another of Peck & Fursman's stage presentations, *Daniel Boone*. The role would change her life, for here, the petite, gray-eyed beauty with the 17-inch waist would meet the young, handsome man who would become her husband, James Deer. Not only did she meet her intended, she met his entire family, as Chief Running Deer was also performing with Peck & Fursman in *Daniel Boone*.

On November 18, 1889, at the age of 18, she married James D. Deer (Jim as he was known) who was 24 years old. Georgette

Georgette Osborne Deer, c. 1890.

gave up her British identity and became Native American when she married Jim, under the Indian Acts of both the United States and Canada. She traveled not with a passport, but with letters as a ward of the United States.

Jim was the love of her life; she would adore him until the day she died. They were truly a loving and devoted couple.

Two years later, on November 2, 1891, a daughter was born. The name Ester Louise Georgette Deere was recorded on her birth certificate. At that time James and Georgette were living at 164th Street and Morris Avenue in New York, near Yankee Stadium in the Bronx.

According to the Certificate of Birth, Georgette was going by the moniker of "Georgie," and the family name spelling being used was "Deere." The child would not use that spelling of her name later in life, but instead used "Esther G. Deer" or "Esther Deer" on her legal documents.

After Esther was born, Georgette continued to appear with her husband in his traveling Indian troupe as a trick rider and theatrical performer. According to The Circus Historical Society, in the biographical dictionary, *Olympians of the Sawdust Circle*, Georgia, as she was called, was featured in a chase for a bride and was considered an excellent rough rider.

Scene from Daniel Boone. *James Deer (right), shaking hands with Josie Cohan to the right of an unidentified cast member; George Cohan, John Deer, and an unidentified cast member. Seated: Princess White Deer and Georgette Deer.*

CHAPTER TWO
Wild West Shows

DANIEL BOONE—INDIANS OF THE PAST
"Running Deer and his family were the first American Indians to give public exhibitions with P. T. Barnum," Esther wrote in her notes. "The Deer Family was the original *Daniel Boone Company* with Peck & Fursman. Jack Crawford, known throughout the country as the 'Poet Scout,' played the hero role, Daniel Boone; Mrs. Jerry Cohan played the leading lady, Susie Boone; and her daughter, Josie Cohan, played the little girl, Lily. Jerry Cohan played the comedic parts. Little George M. Cohan played the drums and did some fancy snare drumming. The Cohan Family, also known as 'The Cohan Merrimakers,' and the Deer Family of Indians made the *Daniel Boone Company* a great realistic and educational drama played which played many seasons and with much success." After Mrs. Cohan left the cast, Georgette succeeded her in the role of Susie Boone.

Captain Jack Crawford, the noted "Poet Scout," was chief of the scouts under General Custer at the time of the massacre. Crawford was on his way to the General's headquarters when the attack took place. Born John Wallace Crawford in Ireland in 1847, he learned to read and write while in the hospital recovering from wounds sustained in the Civil War. He later became known as a writer of plays and western stories.

On the Trail or Daniel Boone was reported by many newspapers across the country to be one of the best border dramas

Scene from Daniel Boone. *Left to Right: Princess White Deer, Georgette Deer (with tomahawk), and Josie Cohan.*

presented in theaters. Set in the late 1700s, the play was based on the life and history of "The Settler of Kentucky." It was not commonly known as a border drama, for while it was necessarily full of exciting scenes, it lacked bloodshed and wild, sensational moments. Instead, it was a playful domestic comedy on the bright side of the life of Daniel Boone.

The company was considered an excellent one throughout and theirs the best depiction of pioneer life of a hundred years ago. The Indians, portrayed as a band of Shawnee, were a pleasing feature along with the horses, donkey, and wild animals. Captain Crawford was considered a genuine surprise as "stars" of his class were more about their reputation and "blank cartridges" than the ability to act. Captain Crawford had genuine ability as an actor. "The bowie knife combat in the climax of the second act," the *Wilmington Gazette* reported, "between 'Daniel Boone' and 'Blackfish' the Indian chief, is a most realistic piece of stage business."

The special scenery, beautiful horses, and all the necessities for the production were transported by special palace cars owned by Peck & Fursman. The routine of arriving in a new city for a two-day engagement consisted of a street parade at noon to announce their arrival, with a matinee performance at 2:30 p.m., a grand band concert at 7:00, and an evening performance at 8:00.

Putting on the play was not without its trials and tribulations. Living and working in close proximity is not possible without the occasional difference of opinion or family quarrel. When this life is also in the public eye, it can unfortunately escalate from backstage to front-page news. Then, as now, the paparazzi and press are there to exploit transgressions.

Such was the case in Sandusky, Ohio, in 1888, backstage of this traveling border drama. Jim, John, and Mary's husband, Charles William, were quarreling among themselves in the dressing room, when the stage manager, John Ungerer, entered.

Their voices had reached the ears of the audience who waited patiently for the curtain to rise. John Ungerer by all accounts interfered in the backstage drama, which caused the brothers to unite and turn their anger on him. Someone fired a shot at Ungerer. Someone threw a tomahawk at him. Ungerer fired in return but was forced to retreat. Mrs. Ungerer grabbed her husband's pistol and discharged a blank cartridge in the face of one of the men who in turn fired at her three times. She was slightly wounded.

Meanwhile the audience was hearing whoops and a woman's battle cry at full pitch. The spectators couldn't distinguish who was wrestling on the floor of the dressing room. Was it Mr. Ungerer with the brothers, or Mrs. Ungerer? The rapid discharge of pistols and the spray of bullets against the walls of the theater caused the crowd to stampede; as one reporter recounted, it "rose as one woman and fled."

Four policemen removed the Deer men to a neighboring station house. In thirty minutes, the theater's houselights were extinguished.

The story was front-page news in New York newspapers, which alleged that two of the brothers were jealous of the "Star Indian." *The Brooklyn Daily Eagle* called it "Wild Warfare;" *The Evening Telegram* wrote "The Realistic Drama" and "Hired Redmen Shoot for Keeps at Sandusky." "They Had a Real Fight," wrote the *Rochester Democratic Chronicle*; and *The Auburn Bulletin* called them "Quarrelsome Indians." The audience thought it was the best border drama they would ever see.

Perhaps to end their quarrel the three should have gone into the woods and set up their sticks, as taught by stories they learned as children, and left their quarrel there. Later they would return when the moon had passed to see if their sticks were leaning to the rising or the setting sun, to show who was right or who was wrong...or to see if their sticks had fallen down, whereby no one would win the argument; if in a moon's time they would even remember it.

Even Jack Crawford would become headline fodder in newspapers across northern New York State. There were explosive articles on how he fought a genuine knife duel onstage with Chief Running Deer. The papers all reported that the Chief was drunk during the performance of January 21, 1889, at the Standard Theatre in Chicago.

While playing the duel scene, Crawford should have taken the knife; instead, Chief Running Deer refused to give it up, and a hard and terrible fight ensued, filled with vicious lunges with knives before an audience.

Crawford did get the upper hand, and his knife made contact a few times, pricking Chief Running Deer in his side. Crawford threatened to kill him if he made any further threatening demonstrations.

Chief Running Deer fled after the play, and the police made a cursory search for him. Nothing came of the skirmish, except maybe another feather in Crawford's hat of tales. It was here that the family separated. Chief Running Deer traveled and performed with medicine shows, and his two oldest sons branched out on their own with Daniel Boone. Chief Running Deer was performing with John Robinson's Circus by February of that year.

A COPYRIGHTED ACT

In addition to the *Indians of the Past* act, the sons of Running Deer created a rough-riding act that they thought so good that on August 17, 1892, brothers John and James Deer copyrighted the words "Indian Riding" (Library of Congress No 7394). They further published the following news articles:

> **"The Famous Deer Brothers Champion**
> **Indian Trick Rider of the World**
> **Assisted by the Equestrian Wonder**
> **Georgie Deer"**
> **Warning! Imitators Beware!**

To all Wild West Riders: the act of trick riding, which we have performed for several years past at the principal parks, summer resorts and circuses, is our own original act, duly protected by law and copyrighted. A printed synopsis of the act has been deposited with the Librarian of Congress. Through our attorney, W. R. Perce of Providence, R.I., anybody attempting to perform in public any part of the act or using our title will be prosecuted to the full extent of the law.

James D. Deer

John J. Deer, Jr.

"Champion Indian Trick Riders of the World."

The greatest and only attraction of the kind before the public, the marvel of exploits of untaught natural horsemanship. We are the originators of this act, and it is the only copyrighted riding act in the country.

The contestants engage in the following feats of horsemanship, while the horses are running at full speed, straight away, or as they please, over the field.

The riders pick up objects from the ground while bending forward or backward from their horses.

The riders ride full length upon the sides of their horses, clinging on by hand, with their heads extended toward the horses heads, and then with their feet extended toward the horses' head.

The riders ride standing on saddle,

The riders stand on head on saddle facing first to the front and then to the rear.

The riders balance themselves on knee or haunches of horses, one leg up.

The riders hang by one leg from horn of saddle, head toward the ground.

The riders vault from their horses to the ground and back into saddle, making a half turn on side of horse.

The riders drop backward from saddle, making a full turn, with back against horse.

The riders vault from saddle to side of horse on the ground and leap clear over the horse to the ground on the opposite side of horse, while at full speed.

In conjunction with Georgie Deer (Wild Rose), a dashing lady Rough Rider, picking up objects, she also performs the difficult feat of jumping from one horse to another at full speed in the chase for a bride and many other difficult feats.

We have a host of notices and references too numerous to mention.

We are always prepared to negotiate with responsible managers throughout the country, at the principal summer resorts, circuses, agriculture associations, parks &c. We can always furnish a Historical Wild West at short notice, and guarantee the show first-class in every respect.

Permanent address, *N. Y. Clipper.*

Either of these features can be engaged separately.

James D. Deer.

Georgette Deer was absolutely fearless; it seems she had a native spirit despite her European ancestry, and took to rough riding as if she was born to it.

The Race for the Bride

The riders ride standing on saddle. The riders then stand on their heads on the saddle, facing first to the front and then to the rear. The riders then balance themselves on knee or haunches of the horse with one leg up. Next the riders hang by one leg from the horn of the saddle, with their head facing toward the ground. Then the riders vault from their horses to the ground and back into the saddle, making a half turn on the side of the horse.

Next, the riders drop backward from the saddle making a full turn with their back against the horse. Finally the riders vault from the saddle to the side of the horse on the ground and leap clear over the horse to the ground on the opposite side of the horse while traveling at full speed. At the conclusion of the competitive trial, the Chief awards the maiden to the more skillful rider.

WALTER MAIN

From 1890 to 1893 "The Famous Deer Brothers, Champion Trick Riders of the World" performed with Walter Main's Circus. Walter Main wrote from Millville, New Jersey, on June 28, 1890:

> If James Deer, wife, and brother wish to join my show September 1 by giving two weeks notice, they can do so and their contract be continued and should they close the season I will pay them the two weeks salary retained.
> W. L. Main

Walter Main was the son of circus proprietor, William Main, of Main & Hilliard. When horse-drawn streetcars were being replaced by electric trolleys, Walter sent his father to Cleveland to buy horses for the show. William returned with 20 of them, purchased for the sum of $200. With this stud of trolley horses, Walter Main launched his circus. Each year the circus grew bigger and better. In 1891 the show went to rail travel, with thirteen 60-foot circus cars; in 1892 the circus toured with its first three-ring show; and 1893 was a peak year, with two rings and a center platform, until a train wreck nearly demolished the show on May 30. The brakemen lost control coming down the mountain near Tyrone, Pennsylvania, and a pile-up occurred at Vail Station. Damage was estimated between $100,000 and $200,000. Seventeen cars had jumped the tracks, killing six men and injuring 20. The loss of animals was great. Nevertheless, the show was back on the road in eight days. The opening performance in Tyrone was a sensation due to public sympathy. License and lot fees were waived, and the Elks Club hosted a banquet for the entire circus.

The "Under the White Tents" column of the *New York Clipper* a few years later had these notes to report about Walter Main's circus: "James Deer, a long-hair Wild West Indian rider known with the Main Circus as 'Kick-a hole-in the-sky' was wildly thrown the other night by the brake wheel of his sleeper, which suddenly spun in the air, landing him on the car steps. He was falling head first from the train when caught by Frank Monroe the double somersault leaper." Ed Rillings, the stilt clown, had an equally close call.

THE GREAT TRAIN ROBBERY

In 1903, The Thomas A. Edison Company produced a movie entitled *The Great Train Robbery*, based partly on a play by Scott Marble. The movie, filmed in New Jersey, faithfully reenacted a genuine "hold-up" made famous by bandits in the west. The eleven-minute movie is considered one of the superior motion pictures ever made.

Justus D. Barnes, who played the head bandit, Walter Cameron, who played the sheriff, and G. M. Anderson, who played the slain passenger, a tenderfoot, and a robber, are the only cast members listed in the credits. Chief Running Deer and John, James, and Georgette Deer, although they did not receive credit, did appear in the movie along with many unnamed others. None of the facial features of the men in the cast can be clearly made out, as this movie has no close-ups, and several of them wear bandanas around their faces. Undoubtedly the Deer men are among the rough riders in the woodland scenes. It is Georgette who can be clearly made out in the eleventh scene, where a typical western dance hall sequence is being played out and a number of men and women are performing a lively quadrille. She wears her soon to be a trademarked, rakish wide-awake hat. Her hip-length hair flows behind her.

Esther grew up as the family was performing around the

United States. Work was plentiful for a family enterprise that was able to furnish a first-class historical Wild West show, even on short notice. When the season ended, they lived in Hogansburg, New York, not far from Grandfather Running Deer. Soon they would be performing around the world, and Esther would be playing a much bigger role.

What child wouldn't love growing up playing with her parents and other adults, acting out stories, wearing costumes, and receiving the applause and attention of strangers who came to see them, some of them royalty? This was way better than having a tree house or a playroom to oneself, and dreaming.

Esther wrote that she remembered when she was ten years old, seeing Calamity Jane on the Midway at the 1901 Pan-American Exposition held in Buffalo, New York. The official photographer of the Exposition, C. O. Arnold, had snapped the young Esther Deer with a Winnebago boy. Arnold also photographed her grandfather, Running Deer, and his troupe, posed before the Six Nation's Iroquois stockade exhibit. Running Deer was 62.

QUEEN OF THE HIGHWAY

Two reviews of *Queen of the Highway* appeared in newspapers, one while it played at the Colonial Theatre and the other on January 25, 1903, in the *Rochester Democrat and Chronicle*, during its run at the Baker Theater. On January 8, in Poughkeepsie, New York, the show was featured in a free Wild West exhibition at noon in front of the Opera House. *The Clipper* reported on January 31 that *Queen of the Highway* played to over 2,400 people and on January 17 broke house record sales at the Grand Opera House in Akron.

The play is described as a "picturesque drama of western life crowded with emotional and dramatic incidents;" a play that showcased real Indians, trained horses, savage wolves, dogs, and cowboys. Boasting thrilling and startling acts involving stagecoaches, bandits, and highwaymen, the show fully satisfied the audience's appetite for sensationalism. The *Clipper* critic called it an excellent entertainment of its kind, of hair-raising realistic action, of a knife duel, Indian War Dances, a highway robbery, a fight with wolves, and a daring rescue from the bottom of the canyon, all enhanced by the scenic display. There was also a measure of comedy centering on the fortunes and misfortunes of Cohen, a Hebrew leader among the Indians.

The Colonial Theatre review included a synopsis of scenes:

> Act I—The Post Station at Laughing Hollow. Where the stage road ends and the daring pony express rider takes Uncle Sam's mail with government dispatches and gallops away over the rough trails towards the setting sun.
> Act II—Interior of stable at Post Station. Where the express rider's pony brings proof of a tragedy.
> Act III—(Curtain will remain down one minute between Scenes 1 and 2, also between Scenes 2 and 3).
> Scene 1—Echo Canyon, where Bob fights for his life and is saved from hungry wolves by Rainbow.
> (Little White Deer in specialties.)
> Scene 2—Interior of the Wild Horse Tavern. Bob's return.
> Scene 3—Shows the interior of Belle Diamond's lodge on Lookout Mountain, the rendezvous of highwaymen. Plans of the hold-up. The torture of Jess. The burning of Manatolum.
> Act IV—Scene 1—Camp of the Sioux. The fight between Rainbow and Jess.
> Scene 2—Hell's Kitchen. In the valley of the Redwood. The hold-up.

The cast included Georgette, under the name "Georgia Deer," as Aille; her husband, Jim, as Standing Bear; and her younger brother-in-law, George, as Red Fox. Her 12-year-old daughter, Esther, under the name "Little White Deer," sang a specialty number between Scenes One and Two of Act Three.

Georgette did not play the strenuous role of the leading character, Belle Diamond, the bandit queen. That part was played by Charlotte Severson, who carried the image of beauty and refinement to the play's tragic finale. The bandit queen is a runaway wife masquerading in male attire as a highwayman, and in the end is shot by her husband, a government officer, in a case of mistaken identity; he believed her to be the man who ruined his life.

Georgette played the heroine of the story, Aille; the hero, Bob Sherwood, was played by Mr. Sharkey. In the review of the performance at the Colony Theater, their performances were well taken; a special note was added about the pleasing specialty in the song and dance line rendered by Esther Deer.

TEXAS JACK'S WILD WEST SHOW—SOUTH AFRICA

Esther's imagination was captured when the family traveled abroad as part of Texas Jack's Wild West Show in 1903. They would be performing in South Africa with their show, *Daniel Boone, Indians of the Past.*

John Burwell "Texas Jack" Omohundro left home in his early teens and traveled to Texas, where he became a skilled cowboy. In 1861, he entered the Confederate service as a courier and scout, although too young to enlist. By 1864 he had enlisted and served as runner, scout, and spy.

In 1866, with the Civil War over, he resumed his life as a Texas cowboy. On one of his cattle drives across Arkansas he was bestowed the moniker "Texas Jack" by the grateful citizens of Tennessee, who were suffering from a meat shortage.

On another drive, he rescued a small child whose parents had been killed in an Indian raid. The boy became known as

Texas Jack Jr. and went on to lead, in his adopted father's name, Texas Jack's Wild West Show and Circus in 1903.

Texas Jack Omohundro was a well-known scout when on December 17, 1872, he appeared in a dime-store drama by Ned Buntline called *The Scouts of the Prairie*, alongside the 26-year-old Buffalo Bill Cody.

The next year Buffalo Bill organized his own show, the Buffalo Bill Combination, and performed *Scouts of the Plains* with a cast that also included Buffalo Bill, Texas Jack, and Wild Bill Hickok. Texas Jack would also participate, with Buffalo Bill, as a hunting guide in the highly publicized royal hunt of Grand Duke Alexis of Russia under Lt. Colonel Custer in 1872. Wild Bill and Texas Jack would then leave the show to pursue their own careers in Wild West shows.

Texas Jack Jr. recruited most of his native entertainers from Kahnawake. He chartered the *S.S. Gascon* and sailed across the Atlantic for South Africa in 1903 with his Texas Jack's Wild West Show and Circus; they spent thirty days at sea.

Texas Jack's Wild West Show, South Africa, 1903. Left to right: Princess White Deer (on horseback), Georgette Deer, James Deer, and John Deer.

Esther wrote that:

> The first land sighted after leaving New York was St. Helena where Napoleon was kept a prisoner. After crossing the equator, Nubians came on board and a good size tank of water was put up with all kinds of sea creatures swimming around. A little later, the ship provided the passengers with a medal commemorating Texas Jack Wild West on the face and the date that the ship had passed the official point of going over the equator on the other side.
>
> Arriving at Cape Town were hundreds of people to see us get off the ship. Father had made all our costumes by hand; they were beautiful. We were the first American Indians to appear in South Africa. I received gifts. One gift, a pretty green and red turtle, was given to me by a native South African. We stayed overnight in Cape Town, then two days along the land we traveled by train to East London where Texas Jack's Wild West Circus was playing.

The Cape Argus newspaper made much of their arrival on Bree Street, describing their attire in great detail. Jim's outfit was "eagle feathers that fell in one imposing cataract of plumes from his forehead to his heels. He was clad in deerskin breeches fringed down the sides, beaded moccasins were on his feet, a beaded waistcoat encircled his waist, and in his hand was a fearful war club." Georgette, or Wild Rose, was described as "a lithe, graceful lady with grey eyes, looking out smilingly from under a rakish wide-awake hat, her black hair falling on her shoulders and her short skirt of soft deer hides rattling against fringed leggings that terminated in dainty little moccasins."

Esther by her mother's side, was being called Little Deer; *The Cape Argus* noted her round cheeks and black, fringed, merry eyes with her ornaments of wampum. The newspaper went on to describe the "medicine man with an eagle-hook beak over his forehead and the bird's talons resting on his ears; Split Bark and the black stripes on his high cheekbones; and three more braves of the tribe, painted, forbidding, with thunder in their eye and imaginary scalp locks at their belts—Anatakeros, 'Destroyer of the Villages;' Rateriios, the 'War Eagle;' and Atsientanone, 'Wounded Buffalo' with carmine spots on his cheeks."

It was December in South Africa when a boy named Will Rogers, who had a reputation as a roper, came by way of working on a cattle ship. While Will was in Johannesburg, he discovered Texas Jack's Wild West Show. He had his first taste of show business when his talents got him a job with the show as the "Cherokee Kid, who can lasso the tail off a blowfly." He was an instant hit. Will and Texas Jack would part ways after touring South Africa; Will Rogers would sail for New Zealand and take the long way home.

Jim Deer was featured on a Texas Jack's Circus Company flyer, sitting tall in his saddle in a scouting pose.

They were paraded through town in three rickshaws pulled by African natives: two men in each with the three women in the other. Everyone wore their performance costumes. Esther, with a new necklace, a gift from a native in South Africa, sat happily between Josie Cohan and her mother. The necklace would become a treasured memento.

Esther recalled spending the holidays in South Africa and wrote:

> We spent Christmas there. We camped in lovely tents by the big top and I hung my stocking up on the tent pole, hoping Santa would find it. But how could he without snow? It was like a hot summer day.
>
> The Deer Family was a big hit and I, White Deer, was brought over and sang the then prize song "Hiawatha."

Texas Jack's Wild West Show remained in South Africa into late 1904. The Deer family set sail on the *S.S. Gascon* from

Texas Jack's Wild West Show, South Africa, 1903. Left to right: John Deer, Princess White Deer (holding meerkats), James Deer, and Georgette Deer.

Cape Town to London. Esther was kept amused with games and competitions onboard.

Shipboard correspondence from the Honorary Secretary, H. Jones, on the ship's stationary, itemized a certificate that Princess White Deer took first prize in the Potato Race, High Jump, Long Jump, Flat Race, Dip for Apples, and "Chalking Pig Eyes," but only took second prize in Skipping and received a Special Prize for Best in Sports held over October 13, 14, and 15. Another correspondence wrote, "...the Concert Committee had been specially requested to present a testimonial to Princess White Deer on behalf of all the passengers for her exceptional talent, in the concerts held on the above boat on her voyage from Cape Town to London," signed on October 24, 1904. Such were the extraordinary honors being bestowed upon a young lady of 13.

Georgette too received correspondence from the Honorary Secretary, stating that, "The Concert Committee have been specially requested by all the passengers to present a testimonial to Mrs. Deer for her marked talent in the concerts held on the above boat on her passage from Cape Town to London."

JOURNEYS

Their future engagements spread out before them, a decade of dreams come true. In 1904 The Deer Family performed in music halls in London, Manchester, Derby, Stockton-On-Terre, Middlesbrough, Liverpool, Southampton, Bristol, and Carlisle, in theaters named the "Palace" or the "Grand."

In 1905 the performing Deer Family consisted of Jim and Wild Rose, otherwise known as Georgette, his wife; his brother, George Red Fox; and an actor, Big Tree, from St. Regis. With the sketch of *Daniel Boone and Indians of the Past*, they were playbill headliners in music halls all over England, Scotland, and Ireland, and especially in London.

Esther wrote: "We were a favorite and at the time played two theaters in the same week. After one act in one theater a groom would be waiting to take us to the next. The music halls have two shows for three nights, making four shows in a night for us."

In 1906 they were in Hamburg, Germany, to play for two months at the Apollo, then went back to Queen's Park Hippodrome in Liverpool, England.

Of Germany, Esther wrote: "We were a big hit. On closing night the house was packed and also with flowers and gifts for the little princess."

The bookings of 1907 were mentioning in their programs that James and John Deer were veterans of the Lord Wolseley expedition to General Gordon at Khartoum as boatmen-scouts, and had received medals from Queen Victoria.

On April 20, 1908, the Deer Family was top billing at the Alhambra Theater on Grove Street in Edinburgh, with two shows nightly at 7:00 and 9:00. They were billed as Genuine North

American Indians in their sensational act, *Indians of the Past*, presenting a "Series of Tableaux in Two Scenes," and were called "The Most Genuine Troupe of Real Indians ever seen in Edinburgh." The tableaux comprised seven acts: "The Indian Camp Fire," "Princess White Deer in her Famous Songs and Indian War Dance," "The Settlers' Cabin," "Wild Rose and Princess Deer in their Speciality," "The Indians Burning Settlers' Cabin," "Sensational Knife Duel," and "Settlers to the Rescue." A special note was included: "James Deer and John Deer of the above Celebrated Family acted as Boatman Scouts for Lord Wolseley in his Famous March to the Relief of General Gordon, of Khartoum."

They were performing with Col. Cummings' Wild West Show all during the summer of 1908 at the New Brighton Tower in Cheshire, across from Liverpool. It was a big show with Indians and cowboys from the West and wild horses. On September 25, 1908, a farewell reception and dance was held at the New Brighton Pleasure Club in honor of the birthday of member Lew Reynolds, of Texana and Reynolds, Champion Rifle Shots of the World. Georgie, as she was called then, and Princess White Deer were on the Ladies' Committee and the Deer Family contributed to the dancing order with a quadrille.

By 1909 Col. Cummings' Wild West Show had traversed Germany and performed before royalty, joining Circus Angelo, Circus Ceniceles, Circus London, and Brazil Jack's Circus.

Circus Angelo brought *Indians of the Past* to the Tivoli Theater in Bremen, to Badenbach in Germany, and to Dresden. Circus Ceniceles brought the Deer Family to Copenhagen, Denmark, and Warsaw; and Brazil Jack's Circus took them to places like Kristiansand, Gjorvik, and Trondheim in Norway.

It was in Norway that the Deer brothers rode before the crowned head of Norway, King Haakon VII, who was also known as Prince Carl of Denmark. King Haakon took a special interest in James Deer and befriended him.

From 1909 through 1910, the Deer Family continued to perform throughout England with Col. Cummings' Wild West Show. They appeared at halls such as the Empire Theater in Woverhampton, Kings Theater in Gateshead, the Palace Theater in Attercliff and Grimsby, and the Hippodrome in Oldham, Hull and Stoke-On-Trent.

Col. Cummings took them to Scotland to perform at the Zoo Hippodrome in Glasgow and the Palace Theatre in Aberdeen, and to Ireland to perform three times at the Palace in Belfast and at the Tivoli Theatre in Dublin.

It was in Scotland that James Deer and the popular Scottish comedian, Harry Lauder, became lifelong friends. Later Harry would come to America to perform for a salary of four figures, remarkable in 1908, and become known as the highest-paid performer of his time. He would be elevated by to the title of Sir Harry Lauder by the Queen of England and become Princess White Deer's manager, replacing William Morris.

DRESDEN, GERMANY

From 1908 to 1910 the Deer Family Troupe traveled to Luneburg, Neumünster, München, Bremen, Cottbus, and Dortmund.

In 1910, when Esther was nineteen years old, the Deer Family performed at the Zoological Garden of Dresden. The advertisement read, "...the famous Deer Family of talented genuine North Americans will present a series of historic and realistic tableaux in their renowned sketch as played by them all over the world, representing the *Indians of the Past*."

A newspaper advertisement for performances at the Zoological Gardens, Dresden, to be held on January 10 and 13 at 8:00 p.m., and January 15 at 3:00 and 8:00 p.m., noted that Princess White Deer was "the only Indian girl Soloist and Dancer now before the public—on any stage."

Esther and her uncle George Deer, who was 26 years old,

were the "soul" of the artistic group. Esther was praised as "a picture-pretty young Indian" who sang her solo "Rainbow" in English at the onset of the performance. The public praise made this song a hit, as she gave evidence of real talent and excellent cultivation. She captivated her audience with the pantomime gestures and expressions that illustrated her song. Local critics awarded her generous mead of praise.

This introduction was followed by a program representing scenes from Indian life. Several braves dressed in full war paint and regalia attacked an enemy and slew him, removing his scalp with dexterity to make the audience shudder. This was followed by Indian funeral ceremonies set to the strains of unfamiliar chants.

In another scene in the performance of *Indians of the Past*, Princess White Deer sang a few songs around a campfire. The Indian men performed a war dance.

In a scene at a settler's log cabin, Princess White Deer sang and danced with another Indian girl played by her mother Georgette (known as Wild Rose), making merry during the settler's absence; but then they were attacked by prowling Indians on the warpath, who burned the huts. Both women were in imminent danger of death when the settler returned and shot their assailants, rescuing them. The scene was already a "classic in the Wild West Circuit" as the public had seen this type of performance in other western shows, mainly Buffalo Bill's.

The performance continued with an illustration of healing by a medicine man, whose spells and incantations proved futile until he disguised himself as a crocodile and chased and scared the patient with ferocity into healthfulness.

The show itself was based on the Wild West format but with the newer developments of vaudeville. There were singing, acrobatics, parody, and clown scenes in the mixture, performed by the clown Amandus and his troupe from the Circus Angelo; but specifically there were lectures on personal experience of the hunt, the war, and the everyday life of what was known to the Mohawks; and in particular, pantomime. The performance ended with the Deer troupe performing a "genuinely American Cake Walk" which was well received by the delighted public.

KARL MAY AND RUDOLF LEBIUS

An unfortunate incident occurred that indirectly involved the Deer Family. John Ojijatekha Brant-Sero was a very distant relative through Chief Running Deer's wife, Esther Loft, who was also a distant Brant family relative. Her second-oldest sister married Isaac Brant, first son of Joseph Brant, and her eldest sister married his other son, Seth Brant. By calling upon his relatives and claiming the family association, he asked for work. John Brant-Sero was hard on his luck and needed to pay his debts.

A dispute occurred when Brant-Sero argued in public with Karl May over a handbill that May believed was not authored by Brant-Sero but written by May's newspaper rival, Rudolf Lebius, entitled "His Syphilblatt and his Indian." The matter was taken up in the court, and it was determined that John Brant Sero was paid 250 marks to use his name, because he was deeply in debt.

John Ojijatekha ("Burning Flower") Brant-Sero was a Mohawk celebrity, actor, entrepreneur, and lecturer. Born of Ellen and Denis Sero, he was baptized at the White School House Methodist Church. His mother was descendant of Isaac, the first son of Joseph Brant. When he was older he petitioned the Six Nations Council, which granted him money to help defray the costs of a business course. Brant-Sero wanted to learn, as he put it, "the business ways of the whites," and "with a fair knowledge of shorthand and some typing skills" he went to Toronto and found employment as a machine-hand with Charles Boechk and Sons. While there he became fascinated with theater and spent a number of years in "one of Joe Murphy's plays." In 1889 he spoke on the government of the Six Nations at the Toronto meeting of the American Association for the Advancement of Science. In 1891 he went to England, where he spent more time on the stage, appearing in the American show, *On the Frontier*. At the age of 29 he married Frances Baynes Kirby, the 48-year-old widow of Reverend H.W. Kirby, rector of Field Broughton, Grange-over-Sands, Lancashire, England. He brought her home to Hamilton, Ontario, where he lived in a large house. On October 16, 1897, a feature article in the *Toronto Globe* reported that he gave a huge party hosting several hundred Indians, who camped on his grounds and roasted an ox whole in honor of Queen Victoria's diamond jubilee. He attracted the literati's attention with his knowledge of Mohawk language, myths, songs, and traditions. He was hired as an interpreter by the Ontario Provincial Museum in Toronto, whose curator regarded him as "one of the brightest and most intelligent Iroquois ever born on the Reserve." He was elected second vice-president of the Ontario Historic Society and the Wentworth Historical Society. The tenure was short.

In 1900 he went to Chicago with a successful lecture tour. His lecture included Indian songs sung in his native tongue, after which he explained both the meaning and the nuances of Indian music. He was known to recite Shakespeare's Othello in both English and Mohawk. It was here that he abandoned his wife.

Later in 1900 he appeared before the British Association for the Advancement of Science in London; he was highly regarded. But in a month's time, Brant-Sero went from a speaking engagement in Liverpool on "Canada and the Indians," to appearing in Liverpool's police court for neglecting to pay child support.

He described himself as an anthropologist engaged in the "study of mankind" and "principally ... the study of backward races and the American Indians in particular." He claimed recognition by major associations, but found it impossible to make money in England to finance the stylish life he was accustom to. His lectures swung the pendulum, mentioning "backward races" on one occasion and "perfect equality" on another. He was considered dashingly good looking, with a flair for the dramatic. In 1908 he won third place in an international gentlemen's beauty contest in Folkestone, England, where he appeared in "full native dress, with feathery headgear" and "jet black hair, which fell over the nape of his neck."

Yet most of what was written about Brant-Sero, whether by himself or others, was unverifiable, from his attendance at the University of Cambridge, to his stage appearances, to his lecture to the Royal Saxon Geographical Society in Dresden in 1900. The theatrics of his lectures suggested he was savvy of what white audiences wanted to hear and see. Some have said that he pandered to the non-native stereotypes; others have nicely called him an opportunist.

Karl May and Rudolf Lebius had been rivals in the publishing business for years. Between 1904 and 1910, May took Lebius to court 21 times. The matters ranged from criminal procedures over offenses such as slander, threats, perjury, and extortion, to civil proceedings. John Ojijatekha Brant-Sero was put in the middle of the long-standing battle by Lebius, who took advantage of a man who was not only down on his luck, but a neighbor of Karl May.

Karl May probably didn't realize that Wild West and Indian performances were produced and played with a "wink and a nod" to the audience, who were savvy enough to distinguish historic reenactment from farce and entertainment. He had reached near hysterics over the seemingly insulting handbills of Lebius, as opposed the actual reality of these "Wild Indian Shows." He took offense at the program bills' grammatically incorrect writing style of deliberate misspellings, which was a poor imitation of the programs of contemporary circuses and shows in the "Buffalo Bill" style, not realizing that these were examples humor, not of illiteracy. Programs were written and set to print by their managers and agents. May thought they were insulting to the American Indians and saw Lebius as perpetuating that misconception.

Did Brant-Sero's participation in the ongoing May-Lebius feud have any bearing on the Deer Family Troupe's performances? It's hard to say. There were few enough news stories about the performance, and none of them alluded to Brant-Sero's kinship to the Deer Family, or dragged them into the ensuing brawl. A misbehaving relative can be an embarrassment. Brant-Sero certainly was that, having stooped so low for money as to insult and slander his race, his tribe, and his people. His troubles did not seem to infringe on the Deer Family's livelihood. Brant-Sero shamed only himself. He spiraled downward and, sadly, by 1914 he was dead.

THE END OF THE ACT—INDIANS OF THE PAST

It was during their time in Germany that Esther's uncle George became betrothed to a member of the Schumann family, and their betrothal party was held under the big top in Berlin. Jim and Georgette, Esther, and even Brant-Sero attended.

The Schumann Circus was founded by the German-born Gotthold Schumann in 1871, who also founded one of Europe's most respected equestrian-circus dynasties. The name Schumann was so exalted that in the Denmark press, being said to exhibit "Schumannship" was the highest praise. European circuses usually performed in permanent structures and were regarded as an art form. The colossal amphitheatre of Circus Schumann in Berlin seated 4,500, in addition to the one in Copenhagen, and yet another amphitheatre in Frankfurt am Main, across from the main railway station, which had the latest technology and could also fit 4,500 spectators until it was demolished in 1960. Still the family name endures with each generation, making its mark in theatrical equestrian showmanship.

George Deer.

To call Esther's uncle George a handsome man would be an understatement. His exquisitely chiseled features and stance of athletic grace could have made him the fantasy material of bodice ripping romance novel covers, rivaling the fame of the model, Fabio.

George's happiness would be brief; tragically, he would die from wounds received in a circus accident at the age of 29 on April 7, 1913.

In 1910 the Deer Family performed together for the last time at the Apollo Theater in Kieff (present day Kiev, Ukraine) and at the Apollo Theater in St. Petersburg, Russia. Esther's father Jim and her uncle George, now a great trick rider, went on to Germany to join a circus. Esther continued in Russia, working alone and traveling with only her mother's maid, Rose, to accompany her.

Princess White Deer promotional photograph used in Russia.

CHAPTER THREE
A Career of Her Own

FROM RUSSIA WITH LOVE

Esther had a lifetime of preparation leading up to this moment. Her skills were finely honed. She was ready to take the stage with her own act.

She debuted on the Russian stage in 1911 as Princess White Deer at the popular Jardin d'Hiver in St. Petersburg. She was an immediate star attraction, and the playbill featured a full page of her likeness.

Esther traveled to other major Russian cities and was a headliner at the Tivoli and Versailles Vorst in Charckoff; at Jardin de-la Ville–Chateau des Fleur in Kieff (Kiev); and at the Hotel du Nord in Odessa.

In August of 1913 she performed at the Aquarium, an imposing building with obelisk-shaped columns lining the entrance, located on Kamennoostrowski Prospect in St. Petersburg. Theatre advertisements in both Cyrillic and western newspapers listed her as a headliner, "White Dear."

While she was appearing at the Apollo Theater in St. Petersburg in November 1913, Esther wrote:

> One day I was selected to appear by Royal Command at the Imperial Theatre. I learned that I was the only one chosen from all of the other performers at the Apollo.
>
> A few days later, I received a gold medal from

Dowager Czarina Maria Feodorovna (1847–1928). She was the widow of Alexander III, mother of the last Czar Nicholas II, and sister of Queen Alexandra of England, Queen of Edward VII.

By December Esther was in Moscow performing at the Yard Theatre and Hotel Sport, and 1914 saw Princess White Deer performing at the Grand Hotel d'Europe in St. Petersburg in the new and beautiful roof garden. She traveled back to Köln, Germany, to perform at the Shilla Theatre and traveled to Budapest to perform at the Favorosi Orpheum.

When did she return to the United States? It is hard to determine, as her name had not been recorded in any sailing manifest that year. It is rumored that His Majesty King Haakon VII of Norway, son of King Frederick VIII of Denmark, her father's friend, assisted in her safe return.

A BRIEF MARRIAGE

Esther's personal photographs and letters show that while she was performing in Russia she met the much older Count Josef Krasicki, who was also known as Alexis Krasicki. He courted her.

His name is memorialized in personal correspondence he sent to Esther starting in 1912, when she turned twenty-one, along with his personal stamp and waxen seal impressed with the Rogala family crest of the Polish dynasty.

David Blanchard, author of the article "Entertainment, Dance and Northern Mohawk Showmanship," is a primary source of reference for scholars of Native American studies. He writes that Esther married a Russian nobleman while in Moscow, who was then seized by revolutionaries and never heard from again. With World War I going on throughout Europe she managed to find her way back to the United States through

Princess White Deer and Count Alex Krasicki.

Sweden. He states: "After this, she was able to claim her title as 'Princess' by virtue of her marriage and as the only daughter (actually she was the granddaughter) of the 'Last hereditary Chief' of the Mohawk, Chief Jim Running Deer." (Chief Jim Deer was her father).

So who was this Russian noble?

Royal genealogy has no record of Esther Deer having married any Russian royal. That in itself is no surprise, because the marriage of a royal to a non-royal, known as a morganatic marriage, would not necessarily be recognized and written down. The royal groom or bride would just be listed as one of the children of their royal parents, and no further notation of marriage or offspring would be recorded for that person, other than death. A morganatic marriage, though, was binding and accorded all the sanctity of marriage, and could not be set aside in favor of a royal union; nor was bigamy allowed. The marriage had a price, as it did not allow the non-royal spouse to hold a title, and neither that spouse nor any children born of the marriage would be eligible to inherit, nor be considered in line for, the throne.

Clues abound as to the identity of the young noble without a name. He was a Russian prince. He was killed during the first six months of World War I. There are many Russian princes; but only one died within the first six months of World War I, at the start of the Russian Revolution, and that was Prince Oleg Konstantinovich Romanov. He was not Esther Deer's husband.

It was common practice for people to send postcards to each other with messages. Postcards were not just pictures of tourist destinations but photographs of homes, theaters, or the very people themselves. Esther sent photo postcards to her parents from the theaters she performed in, and personal photographs. All but one piece of correspondence from Count Krasicki that Esther had in her mementos was written on the back of photograph post cards. Count Alex Krasicki wrote impassioned postcards to Esther.

March 30, 1912
Dearest Baby,
    Between my and yours [sic] watch we have about

6 hours 15 minutes of difference, where I have 12 o'clock afternoon, you have about 5:45 in evening.

Oh the moon is all agleam on the hills where I dream,
Where I dream, all of you pretty Indian Maid,
And the rustling leaves are singing high above me overhead.

You see dearest everything that has something of you is for me dear and I try to have it—oh dear dearest beloved don't you feel how I love you; it's more than love.

I feel myself without you like a body cut in two.

On October 27, 1912 he wrote to Esther:

Dear little child, I have just come as the fourth time in Scheurmany but this time without drinking. You can believe in that I am a nice boy for you. Yesterday I have spoken with Renda—she asked when I am going to Khorkoff. Here it is very cold – snow. I will be yet 4-5 days. Why don't you not work? Remember that your letters are for me.

On July 28, 1913, Count Krasicki sent Esther a postcard of himself sitting behind the wheel of a convertible car parked in front of a stone house with gothic wood trim on its soaring eaves. He wrote: "Today I shall know when I will be Kieff and shall be with you this evening." On the front, in the lower right corner of the picture he wrote: "It's my house."

This jotting would be the first time Esther would see a picture of his home and the statement quietly acknowledges that up until that time she had not visited it.

On June 19, 1915, Esther sailed from New York to Liverpool on the *St. Paul* to marry her Russian officer, Alex Krasicki. She arrived in Liverpool on the twenty-eighth, as stamped on her diplomatic letters, the same letters she traveled with as her mother's child to Russia, as an Indian ward of the United States.

In a *New York Times* article headlined "Indian Girl to Wed Russian," with the subhead "Princess White Deer Sails to Become an Officer's Bride," three paragraphs relate that she, Princess White Deer of the St. Regis Reservation, sailed on June 19 on the American Liner *St. Paul* to Liverpool to marry a Russian army officer to whom she'd been engaged for more than a year. Thomas Thorn of the International Mercantile Marine Company told the press that when Miss Deer applied for her passport, she was advised by the State Department that she was a ward of the United States. Mr. Thorn further told how Miss Deer, as she asked to be known on the steamship, was tall, graceful, about 21 years old (actually she was 23 at the time), with thick black hair clustered around her forehead and large dark eyes. Upon her marriage in Liverpool, she would proceed to her husband's home in Petrograd (St. Petersburg). Her family was at the pier to see her off.

In *The Lincoln Sunday Star* the article was entitled "Indian Princess to Wed an Officer in Russian Army" and was condensed to one paragraph. Neither article identified the groom. Later that year in November, *The Daily Herald* of Chicago ran a small paragraph with the same information given in June.

On June 22, 1915, *The Fitchburg Daily Sentinel* of Massachusetts ran at the bottom of the column "News In Brief" a very small paragraph entitled "Indian Girl to Wed Russian." Although the newspaper had condensed the information repeated from other June 22 news stories to a single sentence, it stated that Esther Deer had sailed for Russia to marry Count Alexis Krasicki of Kiev.

The Malone Farmer of New York reported that the Count had a beautiful estate in Russia and that he was currently in the war.

After a harrowing departure from Russia during the revolution, and with World War I raging in Europe, and possibly with the assistance of her father's friend the King of Norway, Esther made her way home to the United States. Would she really be ready to return to a country in turmoil, and so soon after the sinking of the *Lusitania*?

As to Count Alexis Krasicki, there is no further mention of him in any newspaper of record. In looking at the genealogical registers of dynasties and aristocratic families, there is a Krasicki family under the coat of Arms Rogala, with 169 members. The family is from Poland. There is no male named Alexis. There is Aleksander Jozef Krasicki (1883–1909) and Aleksander Krasicki (b. 1979).

Esther married her count on July 5, 1915. Although Esther saved playbills and postcards of places of where she performed throughout Russia, there is no wedding license or church certificate among her papers and mementos; and no wedding photo. The careworn wedding band with her husband's name and wedding date was among her jewelry.

She set sail from Liverpool on September 4, 1915, on the *St. Louis*, and arrived in New York six days later. The ship's manifest records her as "Miss Esther White Deer." She had been gone nearly three months and had been in England during zeppelin raids in London.

Conflicting reports suggest that after the count was killed in the war, Esther and her mother, as wards of the United States, had to leave Poland. No notation exists on their diplomatic papers to support this. These papers are the equivalent of a passport as they are marked with entries and exits.

Esther did keep photographs, but not many, that piece together her life with Alex. There are photographs of Alex with his dog in his arms before the doors to the stone house with gothic wood traceries beneath its eaves; another of him behind the wheel of his car outside the house; and a portrait of him professionally posed with his dog cradled in the nook of his arm.

There is a photograph of a summer day with Esther and Alex, their arms about each other and smiles across their relaxed faces.

They are standing before the garden wall in the uncut grass with an unidentified but kindly smiling woman who is holding her hat by its ribbons, while Alex slips his free hand through her arm. Esther even kept a candid shot of herself in mid-mouthful, her fork poised while dining. There is a snapshot of the Count sitting on steps with Esther in his lap, and another of them gathered around a table under the summer side porch. But perhaps the most poignant of all is a photograph of Esther and Alex together on their balcony in the city, with stone facades, ornate balconies and arched windows filling the background. He kneels beside her chair as she sits holding a long-stemmed flower in each of her hands while a cigarette idly dangles from his as they stare intently at the camera, their heads tilted toward each other in the expectation of capturing the moment.

These few photographs are all that survive of their love. With all the documents of the Deer Family lovingly stored and treasured, only these remain of her romance.

When Esther returned home in September she went to Hogansburg, New York, to await for the safe return of her husband. Whoever Count Josef Alex Krasicki was, and whatever their relationship had been, his death so affected Esther that she never spoke of it or of him ever again.

She was seriously taken ill on Christmas Eve 1915, and taken to the George Street Hospital in Buffalo. Her illness was newsworthy to two area papers, but neither had more to say than that she was recently married to her soldier.

Oddly three months later Esther wrote to her parents, sending a postcard signed with the family nickname that only they could call her: "Dootsie." She was in Kiev and it was March 18, 1916.

On July 17, 1916, Esther sent a postcard to her dear cousin May in Montreal from her home in Tonawanda, New York.

> You will be very surprised to hear my friend has been killed at the front in Russia. Quite a shock. Write me

soon to cheer me up a bit. My love to all. As ever your cousin Esther.

KEITH—VAUDEVILLE

After the First World War broke out across Europe, Esther had returned to her home in New York. On the reputation of her solo success in Germany and Russia, she found near instant acclaim as a headliner with the most prestigious stage owners in all of vaudeville, B. F. Keith and E. F. Albee.

Keith and Albee joined forces in the late 1880s to promote "polite" vaudeville, and opened several lavishly remodeled theaters on the East Coast. Both had come from the circus business. They censored crude remarks, revealing costumes, and risqué acts, and prohibited the audience from boisterous behavior such as heckling the acts. By the end of the nineteenth century their brand of vaudeville, which brought entertainers to large cities, was considered high-class, with its beautiful costumes and props. It was a far cry from medicine shows, and it was considered that one had arrived as a performer if on the Keith circuit.

Keith also developed the concept of continuous performances that would dominate vaudeville for two decades, before the theaters reverted to the two-a-day shows in the early twentieth century. The continuous performances ran up to twelve hours, in which scheduled headliner acts would appear two or three times a day. Other entertainers who worked for Keith, although prestigious, found the work grueling and exhausting, with four to six performances in a day; and their only breaks were summer layoffs.

By the 1920s every city that had a major vaudeville house had "Orpheum" or "Keith" on its marquee. Acts and entertainers who sought employment at any of its theaters had to go through the central booking office (United Booking Office) and paid a five percent commission for the service. Keith's Palace

Princess White Deer's B. F. Keith Marquee.

Theater in New York City was the most coveted booking in all of vaudeville.

The structure of vaudeville acts were tried-and-true formulas that provided pace, rhythm and unity. Typically the show was a series of eight to 14 acts, or "turns," that were highly structured. On average, a show had 10 turns, which included any combination of musical numbers (performed as solos and duets), magic acts, song and dance acts, comics, acrobats, jugglers, animal acts, celebrity appearances, prize fighters, criminals, and appearances by those in the news of the day.

In the typical nine-act bill, the show would open with a "dumb act" that didn't need to be listened to while people were entering and exiting the hall. This act used the full stage, giving the audience the impression that an exciting show was yet to come. The second act was typically a song-and-dance routine, or a comedy team performing in front of the curtain while the scenery was being set up for the next act. The next performance would be far different from those that came before it. The performer would be the first star, and the first half would end climatically with this headliner.

The second half would open with an act that set the fun-filled pace of the show and settled the audience in their seats. Next would be a production, often a scene from a play performed by a famous actor. The eighth spot was often a comedy act, which would feature the biggest star of the show, and the ninth act would be similar to the first in that it was showy and action-packed to give the audience a sense of abundance, and to also keep early leavers from disrupting the show. For the audience, if one act didn't amuse or fascinate, the next one surely would, providing a sense of high anticipation throughout the performance.

Variety theater had two levels: "big time" and "small time." "Big time" was "big league" and played in major theaters in big cities twice a day. These performers were in the finest theaters in the best cities that used the two-performances-a-day format. Headlining acts could earn anywhere from hundreds per week to more than $1,000.

"Small time" by contrast was theaters in small cities and towns that played continuously, with acts performing three or more times a day over the course of twelve hours. These performers were paid as little as fifteen dollars a week, later up to seventy-five dollars in shabby theaters. By contrast, in 1919 the average factory worker earned less than $1,300 a year; whereas a small-time Keith circuit performer playing a forty-two week season at $75 per week earned $3,150 a year. Anyone with determination and a talent to entertain could earn a solid, respectable living in vaudeville.

"Small time" was also the training grounds for new acts, or for old timers trying for a final season. There was also a "medium time" where performers made a few hundred dollars in a week in better theaters in cities across the country. These performers were seen as either on their way up, or on their way down.

Keith and Albee were ruthless in their insistence that acts keep their material clean at all times. Warnings were posted backstage in all Keith and Albee Theatres. To quote C. Samuels and L. Samuels, who wrote in *Once upon a Stage*:

> Don't say "slob" or "son of a gun" or "hully gee" on the stage unless you want to be canceled peremptorily. Do not address anyone in the audience in any manner. If you do not have the ability to entertain Mr. Keith's audience without risk of offending them, do the best you can. Lack of talent will be less open to censure than would be an insult to a patron. If you are in doubt as to the character of your act consult the local manager before you go on stage, for if you are guilty of uttering

anything sacrilegious or even suggestive you will be immediately closed and will never again be allowed in a theatre where Mr. Keith is in authority.

Keith's theater managers assessed every act during the first performance of the week's engagement. Sometime between the Monday matinee and the evening performance, blue envelopes would appear in actors' backstage mailboxes. Inside would be a note that didn't mince words, telling the performer to cut a piece of a song or other line in the act. Sometimes there would be a suggestion as to what to replace it with. In the end there was no arguing with the direct orders in the blue envelopes. They were final, and you either obeyed or quit the show. If an act quit, a black mark would be put against the performers' names in the head office and they wouldn't work on the Keith circuit anymore.

The United States was preparing to enter the war and Liberty Bond rallies were part of the nation's visible patriotism. Esther Deer participated in War Bond rallies; she was billed as "White Deer, a bright example of genuine Americanism." Many celebrities of the day, including actors, contributed to the cause by raising money in support of American men's involvement in the war. Esther's participation was not only patriotic, but aided her self-promotion as both a dancer and a recognized Native American.

From an early age, Esther was sure in her knowledge of what made her special. She never wavered in her understanding that her Mohawk heritage gave her talent and abilities that set her apart from other performers, and made her unique.

It would be a reoccurring choice for the rest of her career, that when given the opportunity to perform solo, Princess White Deer would revert to the beauty of her roots and stage Indian acts to reaffirm to her audience that what set her apart from the rest of the entertainers.

Esther Deer was perfect for the Keith-Albee stage as she

was a perfect lady who always traveled with her mother when on the road.

Billed by Keith as "Princess White Deer and Her Braves," she traveled the Keith circuit. Sometimes she was billed as "Princess White Deer and Company" or "Princess White Deer and Her Select Company of Indian Braves." No matter what the title, Princess White Deer was a headliner act after her return from Russia.

Often the billings were prefaced with the phrases "By Special Arrangement" and "Extraordinary Attraction" as a verbal banner; and beneath her name, the act was summarized as "a musical, singing and dancing and scenic production" with "Indians Past and Present." She played such theaters as the FF Proctor, the Poli, and the Lyric Palace in Atlanta. In Roanoke it was the Majestic. At a myriad of other theaters, often named Plaza and Grand, amid cities and towns along the eastern coast in 1917, she appeared each week as the vaudeville headliner, Monday through Wednesday, for matinees and twice-an-evening performances at 7:30 and 9:00 p.m.

Princess White Deer and Company consisted of Esther and a trio of three Native American men who portrayed original American pastimes and customs in elaborate presentations. The *Clipper* reported the following details of their performance:

> Opening Scene: The curtain rises on two braves dressed in resplendent war bonnets and beaded buckskins watching the setting sun. A campfire in front of a teepee sends a soft glow over the scene harmonizing beautifully with rays of the dying sun. From the depths of the smaller teepee comes a native song by a sweet-voiced squaw. For several seconds the silvery tones made more beautiful by the steady pompom of the nearest approach Indians had to a snare drum continue, then an apparition

in brown trips gracefully from the teepee and the audience witness one of the most graceful and weird exhibitions of dancing seen in a long time.

The call of the original American to Americans of today to duty to suppress German autocracy was recited by a brave with all of the solemnity of his people. He emphasizes the refrain; that it is a privilege to die for one's country. The older of the braves chanted a weird song and there was more dancing by the princess who performed with equal ease the blood curdling war dance and the clog of plantation darkies. The act is unusual, far above the average and worth going far to see.

In this week's example of splendid savagery the effect is produced by a scene of old America, with the actors genuine Indians of the nomad tribes that once owned this continent the white man now calls his own.

Princess White Deer and her Indian Braves sing, orate, play the tom-tom dance and wear native costumes. Barbarism in its original glory is perfectly exemplified and carried over the footlights in that final, yowling, mad whirling dance.

The New York *Clipper* gave the following detailed review on September 19, 1917:

Princess White Deer, a dainty Indian girl, supported by a company of her race, offers a novel act of the song and dance variety. The turn opens with a full stage, showing a night scene outside an Indian camp. With this as a background, the Little Princess, who is about 90 per cent of the act, although there are three other members, executes a dance to the weird music supplied by her company.

A DAY IN THE LIFE ON THE KEITH CIRCUIT

In 1917, Princess White Deer and Her Braves performed at the Poli Theatre in Scranton, Pennsylvania, for three days. While she was in town she also wrapped up her work of final recruitment efforts.

On this particular morning she was recruiting for Uncle Sam in full costume. Wearing a performance war bonnet, she rode on horseback through the streets of Scranton, flanked by her escorts from the Regular Army Office. Campaign signs were held high over the heads of the parade participants in their straw boaters, reading: "Recruitment for all branches of the Army—13th Regiment needs 300 men;" "Princess White Deer - a bright example of genuine Americanism;" "Do you join the Army today and prove it;" and "Uncle Sam needs you—Join Today!"

After that, she had two receptions to attend. The first, which she attended with an army-soldier escort, was at the Noonday Club at the YWCA, where she gave a short talk on Indian traditions and folklore. The next was in Providence, where she gave a similar talk, then dashed back to the Poli Theatre in time for the afternoon matinee performance.

Immediately afterward a public stage reception was arranged by the Poli Theatre manager, Frank Whitback, for the ladies of Scranton to meet Princess White Deer. Mr. Whitback had advertised that day in the paper:

> Stage Reception to be held this afternoon directly after the Vaudeville where Princess White Deer will meet the ladies of the audience and present each with a beautiful souvenir free."

Oskomon, one of the braves in her review, presented each lady with a memento of the first Native American princess to visit the city of Scranton. It wasn't long before the critics took notice of this "Handsome Hiawatha Buck" and dubbed him "her leading man," noting his dramatic readings were that of an orator. "And Company" had grown to "Her Select Company of Indian Braves," and the braves too had grown to have their own headliner: Oskomon.

Esther entertained the troops at Red Cross benefits with the Willa Holt Wakefield Vaudeville Company on the Liberty Theatre Circuit. For seven weeks in the early summer of 1918, they played camps in the eastern, western and southern United States. Esther's patriotism and participation in Liberty Bond rallies helped bring her even greater attention, and she caught the eye of Florenz Ziegfeld while dancing at a benefit held at the Hippodrome in New York. Ziegfeld was known to have been captivated with the Wild West shows as a youth. He may even have met a young Esther or Little Deer.

Keith went so far as to take out a half-page advertisement in *Variety* magazine that read: "Princess White Deer and her Indian Braves. The only real American Indian in theatricals who dances and sings. An elaborate scenic production with beautiful music. This week (September 3) Keith's Atlantic City." A circular portrait of Princess White Deer, in a feather bonnet and costume as modest as Annie Oakley's ladylike attire, was inserted in the lower left corner.

She would work for Keith on and off again during the twenties.

A FAMILY EVENING TURNED BAD

At the home of James and Georgette Deer on Ilion Street in Tonawanda, New York, the evening had taken a turn for the worse. Esther Deer had shot her Uncle John twice. One of the bullets had pierced his neck and lodged above the collarbone at the back of his neck. The second struck his abdomen. Esther was 26 years old.

John Deer was in Buffalo on Sunday and returned to his brother James' home after one o'clock in the morning intoxicated.

He started an argument with his sister-in-law Georgette in the kitchen while James slept upstairs.

Esther had returned home the day before from New York with a week off for vaction. She was upstairs when she heard the commotion below and went downstairs to see what the trouble was about.

Her uncle grabbed a large bread knife, he threw his overcoat down on a chair, and started for her; while making threats he was going to kill her.

Esther was not defenseless. She had brought her loaded pearl-handled pistol downstairs with her. When her uncle started for her, Esther ran around the kitchen table and at the opposite side of the room opened fire on him.

John fell to the floor unconscious. Dr. R. H. Wilcox was summoned and the police notified.

Seargent John Kreber and Patrolman Edward Marohn took Esther into custody.

In the early hours of Monday, March 26, 1917, she was taken before City Judge C. J. Knoell in the private office of the Chief of Police A. J. Eliot and was subsequently released in the custody of her attorney. She returned home accompanied by her parents.

Esther had told the police the circumstances leading up to the shooting, that she had shot in self defense, not meaning to kill him, intending only to frighten him.

While John J. Deer lay in the DeGraff Memorial Hospital in Tremont with his injuries, he made a statement to Health Officer T. Harris thereby confessing he was drunk, he was an Indian, he had come to Tonawanda three weeks ago from Chicago and was boarding with his brother. He refused to tell where he bought the liquor or anything about the fight.

Later that morning James visited his brother in the hospital and John laid his guilt at his brother's feet.

Later John stated in an affidavit that he was so intoxicated he didn't remember what had happened; but he knew he had caused it. He further stated for the record that his niece was justified in defending herself.

Two days later, Esther's attorney, Dow Vromon, filed her uncle's affidavit during an appearance before City Court Judge C. J. Knoell. The attending physician for John Deer, Dr. R. H. Wilcox, advised the judge that John's condition was favorable and that he would recover. And he did. With these facts before him, Judge Knoell remanded the prisoner with the attorney agreeing to produce Esther Deer at such time as the magistrate ordered.

The question was raised of Esther having a revolver in her possession, but it was left pending. She was allowed to return to New York City on Saturday and go back to work at the theater.

On March 31, John Deer was operated on and the bullet removed. A week later he was released from the hospital and sent to the Saint Regis Reservation. Everyone involved had decided that this was in his best interest, as relatives feared that his heavy drinking would cause more trouble should he remain in Tonawanda.

The actual dismissal of the case wasn't newsworthy; but a few months later, Esther Deer's spunk was noted in a tiny paragraph in the Lowville *Journal & Republican* that she was demanding the return of her pearl-handled revolver, as it was a present to her from a Belgian prince.

The intimate details of what led up to the shooting never came to light in Erie County, nor did they reach the media of New York City. Perhaps they escaped media attention because the front page of *The Evening News* of North Tonawana wrote "Shoots Man Who Threatens Her Life with Bread Knife. Miss Etta Deer, Pretty Hawaiian Dancer, known as 'Princess White Deer' Fires Two Bullets Into Uncle's Body During Family Quarrel" incorrectly writing her name and her ethnicity. *The Buffalo Express* wrote that she was an "Indian Girl from Tonawanda," listing her age as twenty-one and using her given name; when in fact her family hailed from Kahnawake and the St. Regis Reservations, Esther used her professional name in the theater, and she was a woman, not a girl.

The intimate details of the argument that had dangerously escalated has never come to light. Why Esther felt she needed to defend herself by carrying a pistol and what led up to her intoxicated uncle becoming ugly, menacing, and threatening remains unknown. Esther may or may not have shot to kill; her aim had either been his face or his heart, but she missed. By divine grace John was not killed, nor any major organ or artery damaged. The old adage applies here: "God protects children and drunks."

PEPPY DE ALBREW—ATLANTIC CITY

"Nothing in my opinion will ever again be quite as wonderful, wacky, delirious, and glamorous as the country during the '20s and '30s," said Peppy De Albrew, the dance partner of Princess White Deer and himself known as the "Sheik of Brazil." Together they danced in Atlantic City in July of 1924, making a sensation each evening at the Ambassador's dinner and supper dances. Their moves were executed with incomparable grace. They opened with an extraordinary interpretation of the Argentine Tango. Ethel Battay wrote:

> Everyone had heard about Peppy de Albrew, the Argentine Sheik, but few had seen him in his national garb. He is the most graceful ballroom dancer ever, and made a most spectacular and graceful figure in his rich crimson velvet bloomers, clasped at the ankles. The soft white silk blouse was girdled in a characteristic black leather broad belt, ornamented with brass studs. Over the flashing dark eyes, at an angle, was tilted a black sombrero and all marveled at the staying qualities of the cigarette which Peppy had parked over his left ear.

A dreamy waltz was the interlude after the heart racing tango, which prepared for the third dance, the much anticipated main attraction.

Invented by Princess White Deer, "Deer Stalk" was a ballroom dance, a fitting description of the movements of the spirit of the field and wood. For the Indian dances, Princess White Deer wore a native costume of great beauty.

Princess White Deer and Peppy De Albrew dance together in Atlantic City, 1924.

For the other dance numbers, she dressed in a flesh-colored chiffon dress with an under-bodice of silver cloth; the only other accents were a rhinestone rose at her waist and rhinestone trimming along the bottom of the full skirt.

The Charleston Gazette reported that "Bare Legs Latest Fad for Women–Atlantic City Dancer Starts Fad that Takes Whole Summer Resort by Storm."

"Every neck was craned," the newspaper reported when Princess White Deer walked gracefully through the hotel lobby of the Ambassador wearing "dainty slippers on her small feet with no vestige of hose." Within a half an hour every female visitor in the lobby was stockingless, and the fad spilled over onto the boardwalk.

Princess White Deer told the reporter:

> It is surprisingly comfortable, it really solves the problem—"how to keep cool though promenading." Since Mayor Ender has been so kind as to permit us to bathe without hose, taking late consideration our comfort, it occurred to me that he would have no objection to our appearing without them when otherwise fully clothed.

Peppy himself would not have raised an eyebrow over such antics; perhaps he was even the catalyst of the escapade. For the handsome, Latin-mannered Peppy with his lustrous jet-black hair and a figure to delight fashionable tailors always made more news than any of the speakeasies (Place Pigalle), cafés (Madison Bar, Chapeau Rouge) or shows (*Queer People*, 1934, and *De Luxe*, 1935) with which he was associated. His first success came with his dance partner Florence Walton. Later he owned after-dark play havens in London, Paris, and Rio de Janeiro, and he built a personal following in each place; women adored him. He was one of the leading playboys of the torrid '20s and '30s. He was known far and wide, especially in

New York and Miami, as the "Torment of the '20s."

Peppy's trademark, considered one of the strangest manias for animals on Broadway, was the whimsical wearing of a live white mouse held by a tiny chain to his lapel instead of a boutonniere. The mouse ran up and down his lapels of his bizarre dinner jacket in a happy manner, or perched upon his shoulder. It gave women the shudders. He gave up this trademark in early '30s.

He also carried two or three cigarette cases encrusted with diamonds and other precious gems given to him either by the Prince of Wales, King Alfonso, or Pepe Le Moko, depending on the yarn he was spinning to his followers. ("Moko" was slang for a man from Marseille, and Pepe Le Moko was a French gangster. It is also the title of a 1937 film known for its poetic realism, a forefather of film noir, with gritty realism and subtle cinematic tricks; the movie was remade in the United States as *Algiers* with Heddy Lamarr and Charles Boyer.) Another cigarette case is supposed to have had the initials of 100 women engraved on it.

Peppy was known for such antics as trotting out a donkey laden with party favors at the opening of his café Chapeau Rouge, which has been described as a delightful bit of Montmartre, Paris, in New York City; it was three doors from Seventh Avenue and one flight up on West 49th Street. It was decorated as fruit markets, bakeshops, and wine bistros, with French theater posters on the lobby walls and a tiny bar that just barely fit two couples, and held a "Barter Night" where Peppy asked his ritzy guests to cart along all their unwelcome Christmas presents because the house rule would be "no cash—trade only."

His other memorable antics included bringing an organ grinder's organ complete with live monkey into El Morocco shortly after New Year's 1940, and being tossed out of the Stork Club and barred from returning. He later regained entry by taking the job of air-raid warden for the block. Friends gave him a helmet with a bull's-eye on it. His antics were talked about in the gossip columns for decades by such writers as Dorothy Kilgallen and Walter Winchell. Another of his diversions was putting a five hundred dollar bill in his sock and letting the girls scramble for it.

The blonde and alluring Hollywood starlet Peggy Hopkins Joyce, who had graced his club and joined him for the opening evening dance, was much annoyed by rumors that she would marry him and raged at the news media that she wouldn't be making him her sixth husband. But marry he did! Not once but three times! One of his wives was the musical comedy star Wilda Bennett, who later appeared in *Dark Victory* in 1939 and *The Lady Eve* in 1941. Their battles were tabloid fodder for years, making front-page news in the late '20s. His third wife was Olga Hilliard, widow of actor Robert Hilliard, whom he wed on his birthday in 1937.

It was his sudden marriage to Wilda Bennett that finished the act for Princess White Deer and Peppy, as he just picked up and ran off without a word, leaving his dance partner high and dry. Everyone knows you can't dance the tango without a partner!

"The blue ghost that haunts unhappy Indians was on her trail again," a Miami newspaper reported. "One Peppy De Albrew, her dancing partner, without a word of warning eloped with Wilda Bennett, actress, and abandoned his Charlestoning career."

"Nothing to do but rest and meditate," said Princess White Deer. "When in doubt, come to Miami."

Bored with his retirement in 1969, Peppy ran the antique department at Bergdorf's department store in New York. Gerald Frank, biographer of Lillian Roth and Diana Barrymore, assisted him with writing his life story under the unusual title *Champagne and Vinegar*.

FROM WIGWAM TO WHITE LIGHTS

A mention in *Theatre Magazine*, a monthly magazine devoted to the American stage, was a coveted honor for most stage actors as it was known for its high-profile features and beautiful photographs. In April of 1923, Princess White Deer appeared in a three-quarter page promotion for Keith in the magazine's two-a-day section. Dressed like an exotic dancer in a Hollywood harem, she swirls her veil behind her with her arms in motion, her knee bent in step, her ankles bejeweled in bells. "Royalties of Vaudeville" the caption reads, "The Fantastic Ranks of the Two-A-Day Have Opened to These Adaptable Daughters of Ancient Race." (Below Princess White Deer's photo, in a small oval inset, is Princess Jue Quon Tai, a Chinese entertainer with a flair for dainty comedy and a delightful contralto voice.) Princess White Deer's photo caption reads, "An American Indian girl who is popular among lovers of the bizarre in dancing, and shortly to emerge on the B. F. Keith Circuit with an interesting Indian Revue."

In November of 1924, *Gossip of the Vaudeville Stage* noted that since the announcement of her all-Indian revue for Keith, Esther had received letters and telegrams from all parts of the country offering suggestions.

In January of 1925 she played the Keith circuit again at the Hippodrome, sharing the program with Harry Houdini, who was making his first appearance on the stage in three years. This time she headlined with a native Indian dance revue entitled *From Wigwams to White Lights*. It was a highly successful production; one reviewer thought her dance to the Great Spirit would surely be imitated.

New York Variety on January 21, 1925, ran a very detailed review of Princess White Deer's performance of *From Wigwam to White Lights*. The act ran seventeen minutes. The critic wrote: "The act without the Hippodrome presentation qualifies as an early spotter for the big-time bills," but went on to say: "At present it lacks a dancing, punch and variety, the asset being White Deer's personality and the background. Optically she qualifies but is carrying the sole burden and needs assistance." At least he was kind in his remarks.

Without this review, we may have never known exactly what the act entailed, as Esther did not keep scripts of her performances, and there is no record of it having been filmed.

The act is prologued by a brave who eloquates on "one" about the "Daughter of the Mohawks." The act is based upon dances of the 17th, 18th, 19th, and 20th centuries and serves as a skeleton for double dances of the Princess and a male dancing partner.

Following the chief's address the act goes to full stage.

A cyclorama parts, disclosing White Deer in native costume. She solos a symbolic dance, interpreting it gracefully.

Cards at the side announce the next dance as of the 18th century.

The Hippodrome's chorus of 18 girls follows in antebellum costume for a well-executed minuet.

White Deer and her partner, both in cowboy and girl costume, double a one-step and semi-jazz dance and fox-trot.

The 19th century brings on the chorus in Union Army costumes for a Virginia reel, also well done.

The double of White Deer and her partner following has the pair in evening clothes for a novelty waltz.

The 20th century dance introduces the chorus in West Point uniforms and dresses for a corking, kicking dance and drill.

The Princess in short-skirted costume solos a buck-and-slide routine, which registers as her best effort.

At the finish she is jazzing, with all working in an ensemble finale.

The Hippodrome Theatre was located on Sixth Avenue between West 43rd and West 44th street in New York City. Its architects were the creators of Coney Island's Luna Park. It was the city's largest theatre, seating an audience of more than 5,000 at 14 performances a week, and boasted a cast of 1,000. It featured circus rings and water effects, including a vanishing pool whereby actors exited the stage underwater, and had a moving stage. It was demolished in 1939 when the cost of upkeep became exorbitant and public interest dwindled.

In the mid-to-late 1920s, vaudeville's popularity began to decline as the success of radio and motion pictures gained ground, becoming the dominant forms of entertainment in the 1930s. The Depression finished off vaudeville in 1932, most pointedly when the Palace Theatre started mixing moving pictures into their vaudeville shows on November 16. Some vaudeville stars made the transition and continued their form of entertainment on the radio, in nightclubs, in motion pictures, and much later on television. These stars include George Burns and Gracie Allen, W. C. Fields, Buster Keaton, Charlie Chaplin, Cary Grant, Ethel Merman, the Marx Brothers, Jack Benny, Ginger Rogers, Milton Berle, Sarah Bernhardt, Phil Silvers, Eubie Blake, Sammy Davis Jr., and Will Rogers.

From Wigwam to White Lights was a sensational success in January of 1925, but by March, Esther's doctors had ordered her to Florida, claiming she was having a nervous breakdown due to overwork; she'd been preparing her act for Keith-Albee vaudeville, in which she performed at both the B. F. Keith's Hippodrome and the 81st Street Theatre. Her illness was serious enough to have her cancel her contract to perform on the Keith Albee circuit as a headliner for the next six months.

While in Florida, Esther visited the Seminole Indians and was photographed teaching the girls to do the Charleston, and again while teaching them the art of putting on makeup.

DANCING ON THE RADIO

Esther hadn't rested or relaxed long before she received a telegram from Mark Luescher on March 25, 1925, that read:

> HOW ARE YOU FEELING AND WHEN DO YOU PLAN TO RETURN STOP AMERICAN LEGION PLANNING TRIBUTE TO GENERAL PERSHING HIPPODROME APRIL TWENTY FIFTH MIDNIGHT STOP I WANTED TO PRESENT YOU AS ONE OF THE OUTSTANDING FEATURES AS WE DID BEFORE STOP MORE IMPORTANT ARTISTS ON AMERICAN STAGE WILL BE ON WILL THINK YOUR PAGEANT IDEAL AND HOPE YOU CAN BE THERE STOP AMERICAN LEGION AND PERSHING COMMITTEE WILL INVITE YOU DIRECT BUT I WANTED YOU TO KNOW OF MY INTEREST REGARDS

The next day the expected letter was sent from the National Tribute to General John J. Pershing by the American Legion, asking Princess White Deer to participate in the national testimonial at the Hippodrome in New York on April 25, 1925. They thought it would be a fine thing to include on their bill her offering as recently presented at the Hippodrome, with a few embellishments for the occasion. Others on the bill included John McCormack, Will Rogers, Jane Cowl, Fred Stone, and others. Admission was to be by invitation only, and the audience would include the most distinguished ever assembled in an American theater, consisting of cabinet members, members of congress, governors, mayors, ambassadors, and other dignitaries.

Despite realizing that Esther was recuperating from an illness, they truly wished for her to make the trip north for the historic event. "It is such a genuine American movement that an added reason for your presence is the fact that you are a REAL American," the letter concluded.

Radio stations in New York, Providence, Boston, Hartford, Worcester, and Philadelphia broadcast the event live from the Hippodrome from 11:30 p.m. to 4:00 a.m. Of all the performers enlisted for the event, only Princess White Deer, the opening presentation, was noted.

The evening began with the overture, "The Pershing March," played by the Hippodrome Orchestra, followed by the Keith's Boy Band. The Master of Ceremonies, the Honorable James Walker, announced each artist and ensemble. Will Rogers performed next, followed by the special presentation for this occasion of Princess White Deer, introducing Peppy De Albrew and the Famous Hippodrome Dancers in an American Indian Revue in three periods, 1776, 1863, and 1918.

Apparently all was forgiven between Esther and Peppy, or maybe it was because Esther was initially offered Rudolph Valentino as her dance partner. Not only had she thought of him professionally as a poor replacement, but also she was revolted by the fact that he had really bad breath.

The Prologue was performed by Chief Eagle Horse, the handsome native baritone from Alaska, who had been active in Liberty Bond rallies and in 1917 had stood beneath the statue of George Washington on Wall Street trying to convince a crowd of onlookers to enlist. He had also performed with Princess White Deer in *Hitchy-Koo* (1919) where they sang and danced to the Cole Porter hit "Old-Fashioned Garden."

The first dance number, for the 18th century, was "Dance of the Great Spirit," performed by Princess White Deer, followed by a divertissement (an inter-act diversion or episode loosely connected with the plot) of the Revolutionary period. Her second dance number, for the 19th century, was the "Pocahontas Dance," followed by the divertissement for the Civil War period; and for her third dance number, representing the 20th century, Princess White Deer performed a waltz with Peppy De Albrew, which was followed by the divertissement for the World War period. The 20th Century segment finale was performed by Princess White Deer with the Hippodrome Girls.

Princess White Deer's performance was followed by Van and Schenck; Tom Lewis; Dr. Hugo Reisenfeld's Classical Jazz; Weber & Fields; Anna Fitziu of the Metropolitan Opera Company; Benny Leonard, the World's Lightweight Champion; Harry Fender; Roy Cummings; and Carmela Ponselle of the Metropolitan Opera Company. If the home listener had fallen asleep at that hour, he was soon awakened by John Philip Sousa and the Massed Army and Navy Bands with their renditions of "Poet and Peasant," "On the Banks of the Beautiful Blue Danube," and "The Stars and Stripes Forever"; just in time for Eddie Cantor, followed by Elsie Janis and the not-to-be-missed *Highlights in the Life of General John J. Pershing*, a film compilation assembled by the Pathe Exchange.

A speech was made by James A. Drain, the National Commander of the American Legion, then the presentation address by the Honorable Newton Baker. General John J. Pershing followed with his response. "The Roll Call" was sounded, and the concluding tableau of Miss Blanche Bates in "The Spirit of the American Legion," with the grande finale of "The Star-Spangled Banner" sung by Anna Fitziu.

What a night!

ZIEGFELD FOLLIES

The forbearer of the modern floor show was Ziegfeld's *Midnight Frolic*. Many performers had their start with Florenz Ziegfeld and went on to be stars in their own right. Names that come to mind, still recognizable today, include Fanny Brice, Eddie Cantor, Marion Davis, the Dolly Sisters, W. C. Fields, Marilyn Miller, Will Rogers, Olive Thomas, and Bert Wheeler.

Florenz Ziegfeld was "Mr. Showbiz." It is said that at an early age his interest in show business was ignited when he saw Buffalo Bill's Wild West Show in 1883, and the flame never went out.

He opened a variety hall with his father in Chicago called The Trocadero, timed around the opening of the World's Fair; he hoped to capitalize on the event. He booked the legendary strongman Eugene Sandow as the headliner and went on a publicity campaign of previously unknown proportions. He saved his father from bankruptcy and took Sandow on a vaudeville tour until they parted two years later. Ziegfeld had gambled away most of his profits; he took a chance on Broadway.

It was during the time he scouted in Europe for new talent to bring back to New York that his shows took on the unique characteristics that would be hallmarks of later productions: beautiful chorus girls, a never-ending parade of variety-style musical numbers, and the best talent of the day. He also had Anna Held. He wooed her and her money, and married her, and took her away from Folies Bergère for a mere $1,500 that was paid by Diamond Jim Brady. To boost ticket sales he leaked titillating secrets of Held's daily milk bath, since proven a hoax by a dairy. He showcased Held in seven Broadway musicals over twelve years and created his signature chorus line in the original "Anna Held Girls."

With no knowledge in theater arts or skills for writing, designing, composing and directing, Ziegfeld turned a $13,000 production into a $130,000 profit. His ambition was limitless.

In his personal life, he launched a very public twenty-year affair with showgirl, Lillian Lorraine. Later she and a multitude of other co-respondents were named in the divorce complaint filed by Anna Held. Ziegfeld created an absolute scandal when he did not contest any of the charges laid at his door. His mistress married a millionaire who created a public scene when he whipped Ziegfeld with his cane. Then Ziegfeld met Billie Burke at a masquerade ball at the Astor Hotel on New Year's Eve, where Lillian had thrown her expected tantrum and Anna Held, dressed as Josephine, had watched it all. An age difference of 17 years did not deter the love of Billie and Florenz; they were married in 1914.

With all the drama in his life playing out publicly, he was also known to fabricate bigger-than-life exaggerations about himself. One story in particular, a complete fabrication, was that he beat Annie Oakley in a shooting contest in 1883 when he ran away at sixteen and joined Buffalo Bills Circus. Ms. Oakley didn't begin touring until 1885.

In 1907, with the backing of Klaw and Erlanger, the first *Follies* opened in the style of Parisian revues and became a mainstay of Broadway, doling out annual installments of beauty and glamour until Ziegfeld's death in 1932.

THE SECOND SEATTLE REVUE & ERLANGER DILLINGHAM ZIEGFELD CONCERT

In 1918 *Ziegfeld Midnight Frolic* gave a rare performance, the *Second Seattle Revue*, aboard the *U.S.S. Seattle* on November 7. The *Seattle* had just returned from her ninth round-trip tour of duty in World War I. In celebration of the end of the war and the upcoming signing of the Armistice, set for November 11, *Midnight Frolic* cast members entertained the troops. The program began at 7:30 p.m. with a concert by the Seattle Band and at 7:45, Part I began with an overture, followed by "We are the Bright Lights of Broadway." Third billing was "Indian Song and Dance performed by Princess White Deer."

Other entertainers performing that night were such headliners as Fanny Brice, Bert Williams, and Lillian Lorraine (who had the affair with Ziegfeld that ended his marriage to Anna Held). George Gershwin was one of two accompanists that evening, and it was possibly the first time his name appeared in a credit for a performance. He was hired by Ziegfeld as a rehearsal pianist for the 1918 edition of *Ziegfeld Follies*. Ned Wayburn, dance director, had recruited the evening's talent. He created the kick lines and geometric formations that are still used in musical staging. He defined the look of the Broadway showgirl and invented the "Ziegfeld walk," which made it possible for showgirls to descend steps in full costume by balancing the forward thrust of each hip with a thrust from the opposite shoulder. He personally trained renowned dancers such as Fred Astaire, Ann Pennington, The Marx Brothers, Al Jolson, and Eddie Cantor.

The producers, Erlanger Dillingham and Ziegfeld, united to produce a concert series of specialty revues, showcasing the best of Broadway talent gathered together for a limited time, that was held on Sundays at the New Amsterdam Theatre. Princess White Deer performed in the third of the series held on November 9, 1919. She was second billing behind Eddie Cantor, and was followed by Blyler and Green, W. C. Fields, Keegan and Edwards, and Fanny Brice.

DANCING ON ROOFTOPS: THE MIDNIGHT FROLIC

The *Midnight Frolic* of 1921 was performed on the rooftop of the New Amsterdam Theatre, called the Ziegfeld Roof, whose aerial gardens, located in the heart of New York, Times Square, were accessible by an elevator ride ten flights above the street.

It cost Ziegfeld $30,000 a week to run the show. Salaries for the performers totaled a weekly $6,400, with the stars being paid $700 and the chorus girls being paid $60 for working six days a week. There was a cover charge for each of the shows; the first performance—called *Nine O'clock Frolic*—was $2, the midnight show, $3.

Dinner began at seven for *Nine O'clock Frolic* with no admission charge until the show began, but reservations were required. Dabney's Syncopated Orchestra serenaded the dinner crowd. A $20 dinner was advertised for $3.50 to entice the patrons.

At 9:00 p.m. every Sunday, the *Ziegfeld Roof Concert* was held, with dinner at eight and dancing at 7:30 and 8:30 before the show. The best numbers from the *Nine O'clock* and *Midnight Frolic* were showcased. Princess White Deer headlined the advertisement in the weekly *Official Metropolitan Guide* for the Hotel Association, published for New York tourism and given free to hotel guests. Their synopsis read: "The curtain rises at nine o'clock and the bills are made up of stars and beauties of the *Ziegfeld Frolics*. The best numbers of the new offerings are rendered for the delectation of the roof patrons."

All the while, in direct competition at the New Amsterdam Theatre below, B. F. Keith was showcasing his own type of vaudeville entertainment with a matinee and evening show.

For Ziegfeld patrons, the most sought-after performance was the midnight show in all its after-hour glamour. Although it offered a dance floor and music, the real fun was the audience participation. Instead of hand-clapping applause, patrons banged little wooden hammers, or snapped balloons; they participated in pogo-stick races and talked table-to-table by telephone service. It was the age of the "sugar daddy," and to be seen about town with a "Ziegfeld girl" on one's arm was a mark of distinction among men.

The Ziegfeld Roof was a small roof with a movable stage that was rolled out for special added effects. Glass balconies lined the sides which allowed trick staging effects and a place for the showgirls to strut past the patrons.

The *Midnight Frolic* was used by Ziegfeld as a training ground for his *Follies*, located in the same building, on the main floor. Many of Ziegfeld's girls had their start there, and their first taste of the fame that followed. Some of the talents who also had their start there were Will Rogers, Eddie Cantor, W. C. Fields, George White, Ed Wynn, and the famous model Dolores from Lucille's, who strutted out majestically as the White Peacock, with a trick train which pulled over the shoulders and revealed the grandeur of a full peacock tail. She was an

"It" girl. Lucille was also known as Lady Duff Gordon and was the doyenne of all that was elegant in women's fashion during World War I. All of her models went by first names only (people today think Cher or Madonna were original in this concept). Ziegfeld loved her showmanship, which was considered aloof snobbishness by some, and in 1915 asked for her entire line of models, which began their working relationship.

Joseph Urban first designed for the *Midnight Frolic* before moving on to the *Follies*. His work was innovative on the Broadway stage because he used blue as his base color, which accepted strong lamps and was able to create wondrous rainbow effects.

ZIEGFELD NINE O'CLOCK FROLIC 1921

On February 8, 1921, *Ziegfeld Nine O'clock Frolic* opened on the Ziegfeld Roof atop the New Amsterdam Theatre located at 214 W. 42nd Street in New York, now named Danse de Follies.

The *Magazine Theatre Program* carried the order of the night's events. The opening number was entitled "Face to Face" after which Princess White Deer along with Oscar Shaw, Anna Wheaton, the Fairbank Twins, and a cast of others began the entertainment. In part one Esther performed "Dance to the Great Spirit;" she returned in part two to perform "Buck and Wing Dance."

Princess White Deer would repeat "Dance to the Great Spirit" performance in *Ziegfeld Midnight Frolic*, a more abbreviated version of the nine o'clock show. Her costumes were no longer created by her family. The Schneider-Anderson Company took credit for their creation in the program.

Despite a stellar cast, *Ziegfeld Nine O'clock Frolic*, a revue in two acts and nineteen scenes, ran for 35 performances beginning February 8, 1921, and closed in March.

Both *Frolics* closed in 1922 due to Prohibition; speakeasies stole the clientele away. The *Frolic* reopened briefly in 1928 and 1929.

BROADWAY

Throughout the world, Broadway conjures the image of a street of dazzling lights and live theater. During the 1920s it was alive with energy and dreams yet to come true. A new style of acting was emerging and rising to a level of craftsmanship that the world was taking notice of. Artists and performers of every genre gravitated to New York. The city's landscape was yet to be transformed; skyscrapers yet to be created for the skyline we know today.

HITCHY-KOO 1919

Hitchy-Koo 1919 was a musical review in two parts based on a book by George V. Hobart. The music and lyrics were composed and written by Cole Porter. A. L. Erlanger, C. B. Dillingham, Florenz Ziegfeld Jr., and Raymond Hitchcock were partners in owning the show. It played in New York City at the Liberty Theatre for 56 performances from October 6 to November 22, including evenings and matinees on Wednesday and Saturday. Princess White Deer was one of the principals engaged. This was her first appearance in a musical comedy.

The show had premiered in Atlantic City on August 18, 1919 and stayed there several weeks before its Broadway debut in October. From New York the show traveled north to the Majestic Theater in Buffalo for a week of performances, December 1 through 6, 1919, and traveled 75 miles to Rochester to play at the Lyceum for the remainder of the month, with four days off for New Years and finishing on January 7, 1920.

The cast included 100 players. The 16 scenes were designed and painted by Joseph Urban, Robert Law, and Carmine Vitole. These, along with all the props and costumes, required three large railroad baggage cars to transport the sets from city to city.

Newspaper articles began to appear with the preview shows in Boston. *The Washington Post* especially noted that Princess

White Deer was not included in the list of leading women, and that it was she who came to Raymond Hitchcock's assistance with a ballet of Indian girls from the Iroquois Reservation.

One of the Indian maidens Esther brought from the Caughnawaga reservation for *Hitchy-Koo 1919* was her cousin, May (Marie Kaienens) Splicer. May was as close as a sister to her. On the stage she was known as Moonlight. Esther always had a clause written into her contracts to ensure May traveled with her and had a part onstage in the chorus.

When Esther and May traveled with the road tour company of *Hitchy-Koo 1919*, they shared a room; on some occasions they shared a dormitory quarter with the other chorus girls. Unable to blow off steam after work in the common way of dancing and drinking, which was not allowed, Esther and May took to pillow fighting and raised the activity to an art form. When they stayed with the chorus, they too joined in. But Esther and May soon had a reputation of beating each other to the point of bursting their pillows, leaving a room covered in down for the hotel staff to manage. Such were the milder antics of these "rock stars" of the 1920s; the hotel never forgot to itemize the incidental charges of cleaning and replacing the pillows on their guest bill.

Their reputation for such antics would precede them to the next hotel, whose manager would be sure to place their rooms in an isolated quarter so that they didn't disturb the other guests with their rollicking mischief.

During this time, May was in love with a man from home, Angus Goodleaf, and they corresponded much while on the road. May's career took its own turn, and with her acquired talents shaped to Broadway standards she secured her own engagements on her own merits. Angus and May married at City Hall in Detroit, Michigan. When she was with child, they came home to live in Caughnawaga. The Goodleaf family was devoutly Catholic and insisted that the couple get married again in a Catholic church. May and Angus would have three children: Sylvia, Velma, and Buddy.

When the *Hitchy-Koo 1919* road show ended, May had so impressed her fellow cast members that they sent her off with autographed photographs addressed to Moonlight, telling of their delight in her constant happiness and her cheerful and pleasant manner. She truly delighted all of them. And to them, she was a real trooper. May returned to Caughnawaga with a treasure trove of wonderful memories of her days in the sun with her cousin, as part of the chorus of a Broadway musical that toured the United States from coast to coast.

In November 1919, the *New York Times'* "The Playgoer" wrote that Princess White Deer jilted an Indian groom to perform on the stage, a complete fabrication related to them by Mr. Hitchcock. The article also traced her career, including how she appeared in famous concert halls in Germany and Russia to become a "reigning favorite through her Indian dancing and her distinct American personality" in Petrograd; and stated that, with the Russian revolution, the safest place for a person of royal blood was home in the United States. Whether or not this was written with tongue in cheek is hard to determine. Mr. Hitchcock went on to tell "The Playgoer" that he had seen Princess White Deer dancing on the roof of the New Amsterdam Theatre in *Ziegfeld Midnight Frolic* and engaged her for *Hitchy-Koo*, where she did very little Indian dancing but "she does the shimmy 'pretty' and dances a buck and wing dance that never fails to win the audience's applause." Hitchcock concluded with "An Indian princess gives my support a strange wild flavor."

The same story ran that month in the *Toledo Blade*, and in the *Detroit Journal* in December.

On December 21, 1919, the *Indianapolis Sunday Star*, reported that four performances at English's were scheduled starting December 29, noting that the 16 distinct scenes

May (Marie Kainens) Splicer Goodleaf, who used the stage name Moonlight.

included a variety of colorful backgrounds running from the extravagance of beauty to the lavishly grotesque, and with costuming in line with *Ziegfeld Follies*. Of special note, one of the real novelties of the show was an Indian ballet led by a genuine Indian maiden, Princess White Deer.

The show played the Empire in Syracuse, New York, for three days, January 8–10, 1920, moving on to the Forest Theater in

Philadelphia for four days of performances, followed a seven-day run at the National in Washington, D.C., with a day off for travel.

By February, Raymond Hitchcock was taking advantage of Princess White Deer's popularity, playing up her publicity with a photo of her in the *Chicago Tribune* which emphasized that "strange wild flavor;" with her hair loose and unbound she lay atop a tiger-headed rug, promoting her appearance in at the Illinois Theatre. The same photo was used in the promotion at Poli's Theatre in Scranton in August 1917. *Hitchy-Koo* wrapped up three months of performances in Chicago at the Illinois Theatre, closing on March 6.

The *Ogden Standard Examiner* in Utah reported on April 12 that the cast of entertainers surrounding Raymond Hitchcock numbered in the three figures, with the much talked-of chorus being "forty under twenty." The long list of principals included three Native Americans: Princess White Deer, Chief Eagle Horse, and Chief Os-Ko-Mon of the Yakima Tribe, who had been Princess White Deer's leading "brave" three years earlier on the Keith circuit. It was here that it was noted that A. E. Erlanger, C. Billingham and Florenz Ziegfeld Jr. were concerned with Hitchcock in the ownership of the show. And in the next breath stating that *Hitchy-Koo 1919* was the most effective of the series of "Hitchy-Koos." "As spectacular as the new show is with lavish stage decorations, charming dressing, dancing, girls, laughing incidents and cheering music, it is the personality of 'Hitchy' himself (Raymond Hitchcock) that gives it popular vogue...from beginning to end he moves in and out of the scenes and never lets the high stepping pitch of the performance drop in the slightest degree."

By May 1920, *Hitchy-Koo 1919* was playing in Modesto, California, finishing its road tour. The *Modesto Evening News* listed Princess White Deer among the top billings and predicted that "a capacity house will greet the all-new edition of *Hitchy-Koo* where fun runs wild, and youth and music dance with pure delight. There is no refilling of old bottles or lamps. It is the magic spark and grace of youth in green fields of gayety where music thrills and song delights and laughter flows like water from a rock spring."

Although it was a minor success for its producer and star, Raymond Hitchcock (the first version of *Hitchy-Koo* on June 7, 1917, had run for more than 220 performances and moved to two theaters in the same year), it was a tremendous success for the 28-year-old Cole Porter, for the show produced his first hit song, "Old-Fashioned Garden."

The number was performed as a duet, sung and danced by Princess White Deer and Chief Eagle Horse, the handsome Southern Alaskan Indian baritone, and was considered a popular novelty. In the screen biography movie, *Night and Day* (1946), Cole Porter was portrayed by Cary Grant, and only he performed the song.

But, the instant success of the sentimental ballad cast a dark shadow over Cole Porter due to the show's limited success. Porter did not create a single new score for Broadway over the next five years. Theater critics later thought that the outcome might have been different if Hitchcock hadn't cut the more sophisticated tune "That Black and White Baby of Mine."

Not long afterward, on July 30, 1921, a *New York Times* article reported that Raymond Hitchcock claimed *Hitchy-Koo* ruined him. He testified in bankruptcy proceedings that financial misfortunes made it impossible for him to pay his debts. The hearing was to determine if Mr. Hitchcock had sufficient funds to liquidate a debt of $2,000 due to his former manager, Jack Welsh.

Mr. Hitchcock claimed he was fairly prosperous until he produced *Hitchy-Koo*, leaving him with lots of notes (one held by Florenz Ziegfeld who backed the show), a few pawn tickets, and scenery in a storage facility whose lease was expiring and could not be renewed. Several published stories about him, which he claimed were inaccurate, described how he entertained Broadway stars and musical-comedy beauties at his Long Island home, with moonlight bathing and esthetic dancing on the lawn. He lamented that he pawned a watch given to him by Diamond Jim Brady for cash to send one of his chorus girls, who was destitute, home from Philadelphia. He claimed that his wife owned all their other possessions, including the house in Long Island, the apartment in New York, the car, and all the jewelry.

TIP TOP

Before there was *Life Magazine* there was *Mid-Week Pictorial*. The magazine was first published by the *New York Times* in 1914 exclusively to bring war news and photographs to the public in the form of rotogravure, a process by which an image is engraved on copper cylinders for news presses, which gave a clear and sharp image. The *Mid-Week Pictorial* aimed to promote U.S. views of the world and influence how readers interpreted world events. It appeared in two prominent U.S. papers of the times, the *New York Times* and *New York Tribune*. The lavish and oversized illustrated magazine also covered fashion, the arts, celebrations, memorials, and celebrities of the time. In essence the *Mid-Week Pictorial* continues in the form of the *Sunday New York Times Magazine*.

Princess White Deer appeared in the October 21, 1920 ,edition, posed in her full stage costume of war bonnet, skintight short shorts, and a sheathed knife on her hip. She is standing high on her moccasin-clad toes, arching her body and extending one arm up to the sky, marking the transition from her appearance in *Hitchy-Koo* to her newest endeavor, *Tip Top*.

Tip Top was a musical revue in two acts with book and lyrics by Anne Caldwell and R. H. Burnside. Produced by Charles Dillingham it had opened at the Globe Theatre in New York City on October 5. It was considered a vehicle for its star, Fred

Stone, who entertained the audience with new stunts in addition to his acrobatics, including exhibitions of bullwhip and marksmanship. The show ran for 246 performances and closed on May 7, 1921. Princess White Deer was one of the principals, engaged to perform in the role of Wetonah.

It was a musical of old-fashioned innocence and humor of the kind the public had clamored for after the changes brought by WWI. The curtain rises on the trial of Miss Puff, a fairy who has been turned into a cat for failing to tie wedding knots for Alice (Gladys Caldwell) and Dick (Scot Welch), and Jinia (Theresa Valero), and Tip Top (Fred Stone). Alice is the shopkeeper's daughter and Dick his employee; Jinia is the shop-sweeper girl and Tip Top the unhandy handyman. A shyster lawyer, I. Skinnem, visits the store and informs the shopkeeper that Dick has inherited five million dollars. The two conspire to keep Dick from learning about his wealth in hopes of finding a way to share the money themselves. Tip Top discovers the letter they'd hidden and shows it to Dick; and the rest of the story unfolds.

Succeeding scenes move the story from courtroom, to the exterior of a school, to the schoolroom, to Red Canyon.

The Red Canyon sequence in the fourth scene is where reviewers mentioned the setting and costumes were the most spectacular in the show:

> The Globe chorus, as "Sixteen Indian Girls," dances to Broadway's idea of Native American music, soon joined by the London Palace Girls as "Sixteen More Indian Girls." Tip Top, disguised as a southwestern indigene in braids, buckskin, and beads, enters to sing Keewa-Tax-e-Yaka-holo, a satirical song partly in made-up language, partly in English, backed by the thirty-two spear-carrying women in feather headdresses and long skirts split to the knee.

Princess White Deer performed a startling scalp dance of a young buck, building to the anticipated climactic moment, featuring Fred Stone's latest over-the-top trick. The audience thrilled to a demonstration that started with "Australian whip-cracking as Fred snaps with the end of his lash a cigar from an assistant's face, snips paper, uncorks a bottle, and snatches a wig off the assistant's head, cutting an apple in two while being held in another assistant's hand, lighting a match and extinguishing it;" and ending with "a hundred resin balls thrown in the air and shot to pieces by a dancing Stone with a .22 rifle."

What was remarkable was the show's success in view of its weaknesses. Critics remarked that it lacked direction and the thin storyline was often lost. They treated it as a revue because it was often sidetracked by the specialties of Fred Stone (who played a variety of characters such as a fortune teller, burglar, and cigar store Indian) and the Duncan sisters (who played the characters Bad and Worse, the Terrible Twins).

NOT WITHOUT MY PERMISSION: THE ASTUTE BUSINESSWOMAN

It had come to Princess White Deer's attention that the publishers of the *Pictorial Review* were going to run their March 1921 issue with a cover of an Indian princess who very much looked like her. *Pictorial Review* was a glossy women's magazine filled with fashion, style, and other women's interests.

Esther Deer brought action against the publishers in federal court and Judge Martin Thomas Manton issued a restraining order requiring the publishers to show cause as to why the magazine should not be permanently restrained from issuing the March edition with this likeness.

The *Brooklyn Daily Eagle* charged Esther with being "A Cruel Indian Princess" by putting her moccasined foot down on the throat of the misfortunate magazine by using the spear

Princess White Deer promotes Tip Top *in a photo taken by Strauss Peyton Studios, 1921.*

of statute law. Enacted by the State of New York, section 51 of Article V of the Civil Rights law states that "no picture of any person should be used for advertising purposes or purposes of 'trade' in a periodical without his or her consent."

Esther charged that the likeness was a reproduction of a photograph taken of her in Chicago the previous April, when she was on the road tour of *Hitchy-Koo 1919*, and was made without her consent. Officials at the *Pictorial Review* denied the allegations.

The case was filed in federal court because Esther, a Native American, was from the St. Regis Mohawk Tribe of the Iroquois Nation, the Akwesasne people whose reservation straddles both Canada and the United States at the border of New York, where the St. Lawrence River leads to Lake Ontario. She chose to use the residence of the Caughnawaga (Kahnawake) reservation in Quebec. By doing so she moved the venue from the state to the federal level.

Esther won her lawsuit; no March issue exists for the *Pictorial Review* for 1921.

THE YANKEE PRINCESS

The Yankee Princess opened at the Knickerbocker Theater in New York City on October 2, 1922, and ran until December 9, for 80 performances over 10 weeks. It was an original Broadway musical comedy in three acts set in Paris, France. It was produced by A. L. Erlanger and based on the operetta *Die Bajadere* by Julius Brammer and Alfred Gruenwald, with music composed by the Hungarian composer of operettas, Emmerich Kálmán.

Die Bajadere premiered in Vienna in 1921, marking Kálmán's first attempt at American jazz idioms and pop-culture dances. Brought to the New York stage by Erlanger, the story was changed dramatically, and it was performed under its new name, *The Yankee Princess*. It was supposed that this spared theatergoers from having to figure out what a "bajadere" was. (A bajadere was a temple dancer.) As Indian classic literature was being translated into European languages and being sold across the continent, Europe became fascinated by anything related to the legends of ancient India, much in the way they were obsessed with tales of the harem in the Ottoman Empire and Arab peninsula with the translation of the Arabian Nights by Sir Richard Burton. The fascination didn't seem to make that leap to America. Although it received a favorable review from the *New York Times*, theatergoers lost interest. Princess White Deer played the role of an Indian dancer.

The story opens on the Paris stage where the young Indian Prince, Radjami von Lahore, has fallen in love with the actress Odette, who is starring at the Chatelet in the operetta, *La Bayadère*. The Prince wants to make her his bride immediately as his parents have arranged a marriage for him back home. Odette, however, is not interested in him. He engages his friend, Napoleon St. Cloche, to assist him in his pursuit; but Napoleon has his own problems trying to woo a young married woman, Marietta, with his bragging of world travel, tiger-hunts in India, and his friendship with the Prince. The Prince professes his love to Odette, hypnotizing her with roses, and begs for her to marry him. She appears at an impromptu party he throws at his palace, with roses in hand and apparently under his spell.

At the party, while Odette is teaching him to waltz, Prince Radjami tells her that she will succumb to him. Intent that the wedding will be that night, he calls on his friend Napoleon to be a witness and in doing so, Napoleon so impresses Marietta that she agrees to divorce her husband and wed the persistent Napoleon. In the middle of the wedding ceremony, Odette awakens from her trance, mocks the Prince's arrogant assumption that she would marry him, and leaves him humiliated. Prince Radjami promises that she will love him some day.

The final act is in a little bar in Paris. Marietta and Napoleon are now married. She has grown wise to his exaggerations and finds him as boring as her former husband, who now is smartly dressed and has been appointed Consul to India by the Prince. Napoleon is just as bored with Marietta as she is with him, and he tells her former husband, Louis-Philipp, that he can have her back. The Prince enlists the help of the theater claque leader to stage a scene to make it appear that he has returned to India. Odette is devastated by this news, and Prince Radjami reappears and is assured of her love, as she falls into his arms.

The *New York Record* of Hilton, New York, reported that Tonawanda's Esther G. Deer suffered a broken arm while performing on the road with *The Yankee Princess* in Baltimore, Maryland.

In 1925, this play was performed in its original German version and again in 1927, under the title *Parisian Love*, in a Yiddish version on Second Avenue in New York City.

LUCKY

White Deer's last performance in a Broadway production was in the original Broadway musical, *Lucky*. The show opened at the New Amsterdam Theatre on March 22, 1927, and ran until May for 71 performances. It was based on the book written by Otto Harbach, Bert Kalmar, Harry Ruby, and Jerome Kern, and produced by Charles Dillingham.

Although opening reviews called it a "stupendous as usual Charles Dillingham production" and it boasted an impressive cast of Mary Eaton, "Skeets" Gallagher, and Ruby Keeler, it was a tremendous disappointment. A multitude of lavish sets—one in particular depicting "jade temples, henna ships and ardent blues of an Indian sea"—and the artistry of Paul Whiteman and his orchestra could not save what could not pull together.

The story told of a pearl buyer named Jack Mansfield who opens the eyes of the innocent pearl diver, Lucky, to the deceit of her supposed father, who is really a crook. Jack then falls in love with Lucky, which complicates his own love life but creates a romance that is happily consummated. Additional characters, played by Walter Catlett and Richard "Skeets" Gallagher, run an unsuccessful tea shop in the village and each has his own American girlfriend. Catlett is also enamored of a native he calls Strawberry and has the usual difficulties of keeping his secret attachment from the attention of his true American sweetheart. Princess White Deer played the character Strawberry.

Reviews of *Lucky* appeared in newspapers in Ohio, Massachusetts, Maryland, and New York. Princess White Deer was noted in all of them. Two New York papers ran a photograph of her in her Indian temptress costume. The *Brooklyn Daily Eagle* reported that Princess White Deer had "an attractive way of dancing, exhibiting lithe wriggles that make her endearing."

The best musical number to come out of the show was the toe-tapping "Dancing the Devil Away," but other musical songs such as "Shine On, Harvest Moon" and "By the Light of the Silvery Moon" endured and are still known today.

Unfortunately, *The Best Plays of 1926–27* listed *Lucky* as one of three costly, entertaining musical productions that proved

Princess White Deer promotes Lucky, *1927.*

expensive failures that year. Charles Dillingham had tried to duplicate the success of *Sunny*, to which critics were claiming that *Lucky* was "the only legitimate successor and heir apparent." Not one of the three costliest plays of that year recovered anywhere near the cost of its production.

PARIS 1928

Armed with a letter of introduction—from Walter Kingsley of F. Ziegfeld at the New Amsterdam Theatre, written on August 13, 1928, to Mr. Beth Beri of Paris, France—Princess White Deer was set to embark to Paris to perform. The letter said:

> This note will be presented by Princess White Deer, the last hereditary princess of the Iroquois Indians and a famous dancer who has been featured by Mr. Ziegfeld and Mr. Dillingham.
>
> She is in Paris and does not know a soul and I am sure you will find her very interesting.
>
> Parisians ought to be interested in such a fine example of the Native American.

On Saturday, August 18, Princess White Deer sailed from New York Harbor to France onboard the transatlantic ocean liner, *Ile-de-France*. The manifest for cabin class and second class included, besides Princess White Deer, Mr. and Mrs. Joseph Kennedy, Mr. and Mrs. Vanderbilt, and Dolores Del Rio, the Mexican film actress and Hollywood silent film star who was one of the *WAMPAS Baby Stars of 1926* along with newcomers Joan Crawford, Fay Wray, Janet Gaynor, and Mary Astor. She overcame the prejudice of the "Mexicali Rose" image in the year's biggest movie success, *What Price Glory*, and was traveling along with her maid.

The pioneering aviator Lieutenant L. Demougeot was also onboard. He had just completed the first test flight carrying mail from France to New York on planes launched from the *Ile-de-France* on August 13, and was on the return voyage to France.

It was an idea that combined the steamer and airplane to save one day's time for the mail to arrive. It was done by catapulting amphibious aircraft which were designed and installed on the rear deck of this newest transatlantic vessel. The project was overseen by the Société Transatlantique Aérienne, "the first airline on the North Atlantic." The time saved was in direct relation to the difference between the ship, which traveled about 28 mph, and the aircraft which flew about 100 to 125 mph. To mark the occasion there was a special sticker placed on the outer envelope of each letter that read:

**August–September 1928
First Transatlantic Airmail Link
By seaplane launched by catapult
from the Ile de France
Pilot Navy Lieutenant L. Demougeot**

Although a passenger, Princess White Deer performed on this transatlantic voyage along with Delores Del Rio. It was customary onboard ships when celebrities traveled, to give two shows, one for first-class passengers and one for second-class passengers.

If nothing more, the transatlantic voyage was filled with interesting personalities of the time, including of those who were making history and those who would be part of future history, with whom to pass the journey.

The *Sunday New York Times* in January 1929 reported alongside a photograph, taken by Times World Photos, Paris Studios, of Princess White Deer in her famous eagle-feathered bonnet, that she was an American dancer who was to appear in one of the revues in Paris.

A Parisian news article featured a similar photo with the caption "INDIENNES MODERNES.—La princesse White

Deer danse dans un music-hall revêtue de la parure sacrée de ses ancêtres."

In Paris she was well received, but did not achieve the same height of fame as Josephine Baker. For her Paris program Princess White Deer specialized in Mohawk dancing.

She sailed on the *Aquitania* from Southampton, England, on March 13, 1929 arriving on March 19 in New York. The

Princess White Deer, c. 1928–29, promoting her Paris Revue.

Brooklyn Daily Eagle reported on March 21, "Indian Actress Home" and noted her return to the states from the stage of Paris vaudeville, with an accompanying photo of her smiling and waving while perched on the ship's rail.

The front page of *The Bismarck Tribune* on March 30, below the fold, reported her arrival days later in "Pictures Flashes Out Of The Day's News From Around The World," displaying a photo of a smiling Esther beneath a jaunty cloche. She had been gone seven months.

Bust of Princess White Deer by Gertrude Colburn, on permanent display at the Lake Mohawk Country Club.

CHAPTER FOUR
The Lake Mohawk Connection

BUILDING A DREAM
More than 75 years ago, in the 1920s, through the vision of Arthur Crane and Herbert Closs, the beautiful Sparta Valley in Northern New Jersey was about to change. The valley, once known as Brogden Meadows, was shaped like an elongated bowl and surrounded by towering hills. The floor of pastoral land was broken by wooded knolls, ridges, and a wide stream that wound its way through. With Briar Ridge to the west, the land was more angular, rugged, and heavily wooded with crags and outcroppings; and with the Wallkill mountains to the east, the land rose gracefully in three distinct levels of land, fields, and orchards. In the hues of twilight, purple shadows created the illusion of water and the outcroppings appeared like islands, creating the dream. By damming the valley at the north end, these acres would turn into a large and beautiful lake. It was a revolutionary dream that could have only happened in the early half of the twentieth century.

The Crane Company had built lake developments before at Indian Lake, Rainbow Lakes, and Lake Arrowhead in Denville, New Jersey. With painstaking attention to detail, plans were carefully made for a lake community that would exceed all others in refinement, improvements, and architectural uniqueness. Cottages and cabins would be nestled in the hills, roads would be built, and boats would come.

Assembling the property was a monumental task. The valley had to be owned from mountain to mountain and every acre in between. Twenty-three hundred acres in total were purchased before ground could be broken. Nine large pieces were assembled with several smaller ones. Estates were bought out, heirs were assembled and satisfied. One parcel alone had more than 300 heirs. The purchase price exceeded several hundred thousand dollars, and land values ran from $30 an acre to $1500. Then the permission of the state had to be obtained for the creation of the vastness of the lake before a steam shovel could break ground. In January of 1926 work was started.

Clearing the land was no small task, and huge gangs from the surrounding local area set to work. For the next eight months the valley was a hive of activity each day from 8:00 a.m. to 5:00 p.m. . Smoke billowed from brush fires, and blasting echoed and reverberated in the hills. Tractors, steam shovels, and iron mules worked incessantly. On August 1, 1926, the gate to the dam was closed, the stream overflowed its banks, and Lake Mohawk was born from the source of the Wallkill River that flows into the Hudson at Kingston, New York. It was a slow process, and after 18 months on March 17, 1928, the water went over the spillway.

Construction on the first house was started in May of 1927 on a waterfront lot; it was to be the temporary home of the Crane Company's administrative office. Streets were cut along the level of the East Shore. The ornamental parkway entrance was cut through to the highway, and the plaza was taking shape. Lake Mohawk was to have a beautiful plaza, a business section. and a boardwalk extending a mile across the dam to the West Shore. There would be private bathing beaches spread out around its shores, roads to every homesite, artesian wells bringing water to every cottage, and a country club for its members to enjoy.

Lake Mohawk lay in Sussex County, 12 miles North from Dover, New Jersey, and a short distance from the cities and suburbs in the Newark area. A new county highway, Route 181, had just been put through; but still it was off the beaten path.

Road signs, general publicity, a direct-mail campaign, broker organizations, and newspaper advertising all played a part in bringing Lake Mohawk to the public's attention. Attractive folders were sent out depicting an Indian spirit in clouds hovering over the lake, with children below playing on former native camping grounds and hunting trails. It was a good contrast between old pioneers who lived off the forest, and the new modern ones making their way into countryside.

In June the lake was ready for the general public, and Sunday, June 19, was set for the opening day. But it was not to be; for a steady downpour filled the day, and the opening date was moved to the next Sunday, June 26.

Crane and Closs didn't just arbitrarily name the new lake. "The word 'Reservation' was borrowed from the Six Nations Indian Reservations in New York State. The development now, as then, is referred to as the Lake Mohawk Reservation."

The original architecture was conceived as English Norman, but most of that was uniquely designed by Herbert Closs, drawing from Kansas City's famous Country Club Estates. The potable water plant was patterned after one he saw in Hollywood-by-the-Sea in Florida. Thomas Edison was an influence, with the gatehouses being patterned after his Llewellyn Park in West Orange, New Jersey, and the sunken gardens were patterned after Florida's Coral Gables.

All of this gave Lake Mohawk an eclectic "lakestyle" with clubhouse, walls, and boardwalk entrances created from natural stone and timber. The fanciful architecture of the community embraced English Tudor, Swiss Chalet, Norman, Colonial, and rural log-cabin styles, with beautiful stonework of the arts and crafts influence. Most interiors had vaulted ceilings, hand-hewn beams, a fireplace of river rock, and a mantel made of a large beam.

Arthur Crane's publicity department had contacted Princess White Deer. She became wholeheartedly interested in the story and agreed to participate in the ceremonies that would name Lake Mohawk after her tribe, and dedicate it to posterity. Who better than Princess White Deer to fulfill this role? She possessed the heredity, the distinguished beauty of her time, and the glamour of Broadway and the fame that comes with it. Crowds drawn by her celebrity would see the beauty of the new community created by Arthur Crane and Herbert Closs.

With the aid of Sparta Township, a very attractive program of the coming event was sent out. History was in the making as newspapers covered the story; cameramen were ready to capture the event. A 24-piece band was supplied, the Campfire Girls lent their aid to escort the Princess, the Sussex Boy Scouts were there to raise the American Flag, a crack drill squad from the American Legion Post of Newton was on hand to fire a salute, and the "To the Colors" call was blown by a volunteer Marine Corps bugler. Speeches were written and memorized. The visit of the Mohawk Princess and the dedication of Lake Mohawk was a big event in Sussex County.

It was a success. Princess White Deer arrived, made her dedication, and captivated the hearts of the people.

> Friends, I, Princess White Deer of the Mohawks, bring you greeting. I have come far to name this beautiful lake which now covers an ancient campground of my people. Tradition has it that this valley was once the scene of a furious combat between a war party of Mohawks and the Lenni Lenapes.

Those times, however, are now past. The hatchet is buried and the flag above us stands for peace. I wish you well here and know that this enchanting spot will be the chosen location for thousands of homes and many thousands of your people.

I feel a singular honor in being asked to name this, the second largest lake in New Jersey, and according to the rites of my fathers, I call upon the elements to be kind here—West—North—East and South. I ask the rain to fall gently in season, the winter to be mild, the sun to shine brightly and breezes to blow coolly. May your race find pleasure and health here; may there be many canoes upon the waters and homes in the woodland.

I will now raise this pennant where it can be seen by all and thus I name—LAKE MOHAWK. May you prosper.

Afterward, a reception was held in the Crane Company's administrative office, the first house built on East Shore Trail at the western end of the sunken garden. Princess White Deer was presented with a Indian blanket made by Pendleton Woolen Mills, a replica of the one presented to Mrs. Warren G. Harding by the tribal chiefs at the opening of the Oregon Trail in 1923, where formal dedication was made by President Harding during a tour of the West Coast. The old Oregon Trail was dedicated as a new transcontinental highway starting from Leavenworth, Kansas, and ending in Meacham, Oregon. The blanket pattern was a new one and considered a great beauty. It is popularly known as the Harding design and is still manufactured by Pendleton Woolen Mills to this day. The original presentation shawl is on permanent display at the Harding Memorial at Marion, Ohio. Princess White Deer carried this blanket with her each time she came back to Lake Mohawk.

In honor of her enthusiasm and participation in dedicating and naming Lake Mohawk, the plaza was named "White Deer Plaza" after her; it is still known by that name today.

Unbeknownst to the people of Sparta, Arthur Crane, and Herbert Closs, the week before the dedication of Lake Mohawk, Princess White Deer was in an automobile accident. Despite the heavy rains on June 19, she and her father appeared at Lake Mohawk only to be as disappointed as the people who turned out when the decision was made to postpone the event seven days. A number of children were introduced to Princess White Deer and they found it hard to believe that the woman talking to them in modern clothing was a real Indian. They expected feathers and beads. She promised them that she would be in full Indian regalia the next weekend, which satisfied them for the moment. Esther had just come off a run on Broadway. *Lucky* had closed on May 21, 1927, after 71 performances. She had an offer pending to join another Broadway show, *The Desert Song*. She was living in an apartment at the Plaza Annex on Central Park South.

She sang on a half-hour-long radio program, *An American Indian Idyll*. The program had aired on radio station WGL in New York on May 26, and could be heard from Fitchburg, Massachusetts to Edwardsville, Illinois. This was the fourth time she had performed from the Majestic Hotel for WGL. She also performed at the Roosevelt Hotel with WRNY. She was taking her singing seriously and was under the guidance of a voice coach, the well-known Russian singer Helen Romanoff.

It was spring; she had some time off before her next engagement at Lake Mohawk. So with her father, her Uncle John, and a friend, she drove her car north from New York toward Hogansburg on the St. Regis Reservation to see family and old friends. It was Thursday, June 16; the Lake Mohawk dedication was three days away.

They were a few miles outside of Elizabethtown, New York—about 100 miles from their destination—when something went wrong. The steering gear broke; the car went out of control and landed upside down in a ditch. Esther sustained a fractured rib and severe bruising. Everyone else in the car was uninjured. She spent the next few days nursing her injuries on the St. Regis Reservation, most likely with her cousin May and family by her side at the hotel that Grandfather Running Deer had left her. When asked by the *New Jersey Herald* reporter about her appearance on the 19th after her accident she said "The people expected me, and I will be there." He concluded his story with "such is an example of true breed in any race."

THE FIFTH ANNIVERSARY

Many changes occurred in the five years after the dedication. For one, the clubhouse and promenade had been completed. The plaza was populated with buildings. Originally the lake was intended as a summer club for upper-income people, but soon after its opening, the nation was hit with the Great Depression; surprisingly the lake continued to attract buyers. Bathing beauties at Lake Mohawk caught newspaper editors' attention and made Lake Mohawk "the place to be."

The Administration Building, currently a real estate office, opened on the boardwalk in 1929 with a three-million-candle power aerial beacon, the first in Sussex County, installed on its tower. Smooth roads were paved to every section. Fire hydrants, utility poles, and miles of water mains were all installed. All the lots were sold on the east side.

In July, Lake Mohawk's publication, *The Lake Mohawk Papoose*, announced "Princess White Deer to be Mohawk's Queen for 1932." She would be there as Queen of the Children's Pageant on August 20. The September 24 edition of *The Papoose* recapped the fifth anniversary with a feature story and

Princess White Deer inside the ballroom of the Lake Mohawk Country Club extending the Harding design blanket by Pendleton presented to her at the dedication, 1932.

centerfold of photos capturing the day's events. Harry Callahan had accepted the Chairmanship of the pageant committee in June, and had worked hard to bring the largest number of children and floats ever assembled onto the promenade. One hundred and fifty children and 20 floats were lined up. Thirty ladies in waiting attended Princess White Deer, who was escorted by her father, Chief James Deer.

The procession, headed by the police and a 45-piece drum and bugle corps, moved down the promenade. Boy Scouts carried the colors and country-club flag. The procession continued to the lower promenade, where the court held its place until

Princess White Deer and her father, Chief James Deer, outside the Lake Mohawk Country Club, 1932.

Princess White Deer occupied her throne. The pageant circled the plaza to return to the clubhouse where the police band and scouts took up their formation, and the ladies of the court made an arch of Mohawk flags under which the Princess and her escort passed on their way to the clubhouse, where a program of entertainment ensued with folk dancing by the children's dance class, a genuine *Punch and Judy Show*, a tap dance, and magic show. Afterward, Princess White Deer stirred the audience with an ancient Indian song in the Mohawk language, with its sad melody of the passing of the once powerful race. She followed with an uplifting song, "The Land of the Sky Blue Water."

Photos of the event show that Princess White Deer carried over her arm the Harding Pendleton blanket that was presented to her at the dedication ceremony. She didn't forget that small detail.

THE TENTH ANNIVERSARY

The tenth anniversary was held on August 14, 1937. Princess White Deer and her father returned once again to Lake Mohawk. The country club planned an even larger extravaganza. And *The Lake Mohawk Papoose* had reprinted her dedication speech the preceding June to stimulate community interest.

The Papoose recapped the pageantry in the August/September 1937 issue in great detail:

> There were at least 250 entrants in eight sections arranged for and it was necessary by reason of car, auto floats and a cavalry section to divide the parade into two divisions. The First Division formed at the Clubhouse and proceded down the promenade led by the Chiefs of Lake and Sparta Police Departments. Following came the band, the colors, Chief John Deer

and Princess White Deer in full regalia, and a court of 28 lovely girls. The Decorated Carriage Section led the entrants. then came the Walking Section, the Decorated Bicycle Section and the Children's Float Section. As the First Division passed before the Queen's Throne and took position in the Plaza, the Drum and Bugle Corps of William J. Hocking, Post No. 91 American Legion, burst into fanfare and led the Cavalry Section, decorated cars and floats comprising the Second Division, around the Plaza to their respective places. National, Legion, and Country Club Colors were then marshalled to the center of the Plaza before the throne and preceded to the base of the sixty foot steel flagpole erected at the foot of Winona Parkway (which still stands today) and presented to you by this, your little publication. Your humble editor then presented Princess White Deer with a folded 10 x 15 foot American Flag that in turn was offered by the Princess to the girls of her court. Two by two the girls descended from the throne and opened the flag until twenty-four girls were in formation carrying the outspread banner. To the music of "The Stars and Stripes Forever" played by the band, the Princess and her court made their way across the plaza to the flagpole setting where Princess White Deer spoke as follows:

"Greeting: Ten years ago on this very spot, I invoked the Great Spirit to look kindly upon the efforts of those who brought about this Colony. I asked the sun to shine brightly; the rain to fall gently, and the breezes to blow coolly. Ten years ago I said "may there be many homes in the woodland, and many canoes upon the water." I asked that your race might find health and happiness here, and that you might prosper. The Great Spirit was kind; he heard the voice of White Deer. This valley of my people is now the valley of your people, and your flag is now my flag. Therefore, I raise this emblem over Lake Mohawk, and ask again that you continue here in health and happiness, and that you enjoy great peace."

The flag was then attached to the halliards and raised to the inspiring "Call to the Colors." As the flag reached the top of the pole a yacht cannon was discharged from the tower of the Lake Office and the band played "America." By strange coincidence a white dove was seen by many to cut across the Plaza in swift flight and circle the pole just as the new flag unfurled in the breeze.

The Drum and Bugle Corps, under ex-marine Sergeant Edwin Borgwaldt of Wharton then gave an exhibition drill in the Plaza after which the First Division of the parade again formed and proceeded back to the Clubhouse, led by the band. As the First Division left the Plaza, the Drum and Bugle Corps led the Second Division up East Shore Trail to Columbus Road where it dispersed. Prizes were then presented by the Princess to the winners of the competitions.

In the evening a dance and reception to honor Princess White Deer was held in the Clubhouse at which time the Princess was presented with a beautiful bouquet of red roses. Many members took the opportunity of meeting Princess White Deer in person and congratulated her on the outstanding part she had played in the history of our lake. News reel photographers took pictures of the event which were later shown in Radio City Music Hall and throughout the country.

Lake Mohawk kept track of their favorite Indian Princess, their patroness, over the years. No fewer than ten articles, in addition to the coverage of their fifth and tenth anniversary, were written about her in the Lake Mohawk *Papoose* from 1932 to 1940. A handful more would appear over the next decades.

In the January–February 1935 issue, an enthusiastic club member reported that Princess White Deer had been chosen as premier danseuse in Longfellow's Indian Opera, *Minnehaha*, which was soon to open at the Manhattan Opera House. "It is nice to know our Indian star is ascending, and we extend our heartiest congratulations."

January 1939 brought news of the resident sculptress, Gertrude Colburn, who told *The Papoose* that she had worked with Princess White Deer and created five life-size studies, one of which rested in the niche above her fireplace in her home on West Shore Trail.

Judy Dunn, author of *Lake Mohawk Reflections*, found one of the busts during her research. Which bust it is, is not known; but the other busts remain with the family. With a little restoration, the sculpture is now proudly displayed at the Lake Mohawk Country Club for its members to enjoy.

In August, 1939 condolences were placed in *The Papoose* on the passing of Chief Ar Ha Ken Kia Ka (Cutting the Forest), James Deer, father of Princess White Deer, noting that he was active in the community's original dedication and its anniversaries, and listing his life deeds as soldiering, acting, circus riding and Indian activism. *The Papoose* on behalf of its members extended "its sincere sympathy to his family."

For Lake Mohawk residents, Princess White Deer and her father were more than mascots, they were their royalty.

Then war came again, another war to end all wars. Esther Deer had had a good career run and retired from the stage at the age of forty-eight.

The Papoose spent the following years reporting on the news of its members' sons and husbands on the front, listing the men in active duty, their honors, their death tolls and memorials, and the lucky ones who returned home. The 15th anniversary passed almost unnoticed and devoid of the fanfare of the previous milestones, as the community was caught up in the spirit of frugality and sacrifice for the benefit of the nation, while those who were serving gave their lives for freedom. The 20th anniversary was celebrated in a different manner, and the memory of Princess White Deer was fading into the annals of time, between the pages of the history of the community's origins.

Princess White Deer and Herbert Closs stayed in touch over the years. In a letter written to her on July 3, 1979, he wrote on Arthur D. Crane stationary that he "couldn't let this opportunity go by without sending this material along... thought you would enjoy the June and July issues of *The Papoose* and a copy of page 18 from the March 1968 *Papoose*... and again express the gratitude of the Club and the Arthur D. Crane Company for the gracious way in which you helped us dedicate our Lake, around which there are now more than 2,500 homes... I am filing this letter with your last Christmas card which is really beautiful. Hope you may live many years to continue to send us a Christmas card with a deer to denote that again we have heard from you."

CHAPTER FIVE
Artists and Scholars

THE ARTISTS

Throughout Esther's life she was photographed by some of world's most renowned photographers, whose talent and style still endure. Among them are Arnold Genthe, Alfred Cheney Johnston for the Ziegfeld Follies, C. E. Engelbrecht, and the renowned portraitist E. O. Hoppé, and studios such as Pach Brothers, Moody, Moffet, Straus Peyton, G. Maillard Kesslere. She also posed for C. O. Arnold, the official photographer for the Pan-American Exposition held in Buffalo, New York.

Her form was in demand by sculptors such as A. Sterling Calder and Ulric H. Ellerhusen (and Gertrude Colburn, whose works are in the Peabody Art Collection in Maryland and the Sparta Library of New Jersey, on loan to the Lake Mohawk Country Club).

Esther modeled for the illustrator Penrhyn Stanlaws, whose "Stanlaw's Girl" rivaled the popularity of the "Gibson Girl." One of the most sought-after cover illustrators of his day, whose worked adorned magazines such as the *Saturday Evening Post, Hearts, Life,* and *Metropolitan,* he also built the Hotel des Artistes in 1917 and directed seven films during the 1920s.

A watercolor entitled *Princess White Deer,* which was painted by an unknown American School artist, shows Esther riding away on horseback, her hair in ponytails and wearing a vest of Indian motif. This same motif is on the vest she wears in a photograph with her mother and father in their Wild West show attire.

ARNOLD GENTHE

Arnold Genthe was a self-taught photographer who emigrated from Germany to San Francisco. He became famous for photographing Chinese immigrants in that city's Chinatown, and for photographing the aftermath and destruction caused by the earthquake in 1906, which also destroyed his own studio, which he later rebuilt. Genthe was mainly known for his portraits, and he had cultivated society matrons as clientele.

In 1910 Genthe moved to New York City, where he lived until his death. He worked primarily in portraiture and with modern dancers. His clientele included Anna Pavlova, Isadora

Princess White Deer, photographed by Arnold Genthe.

Duncan, Ruth St. Denis, and Martha Graham, as well as artists such as the actress Sarah Bernhardt; the writer Sinclair Lewis; film stars John Barrymore, Greta Garbo, and Mary Pickford; and politicians such as President Woodrow Wilson, Theodore Roosevelt, and John D. Rockefeller.

Although considered a ladies' man, Arnold Genthe really liked women, and most opinions of the time agree that he had a true appreciation for their beauty and intellect.

On October 14, 1919, Princess White Deer joined the ranks of those he had photographed. His portraits of her capture three distinct expressions. In the first portrait, Esther is in street clothes, her long, dark hair parted on the right and cascading over her shoulders, obscuring the design of her blouse to her waist, as she looks off into the distance with just a slight a tilt of her head. In the second portrait she is in her Indian stage costume; her bonnet, the full feather headdress, frames her small, delicately portrayed face. In the third portrait, Princess White Deer is the dancer caught in motion, almost as if this were a freeze-frame taken from a sequence filmed in a motion picture. Her costume is scanty: a loincloth and a breast plate, halter top with arm bracelets, and beaded knee garters, with a smaller bonnet of feathers atop her head. All of these works are preserved in the Library of Congress Prints and Photographs Division.

COOPER UNION WOMAN'S ART SCHOOL

Princess White Deer was much in demand as a model. Cooper Union, a university "for the Advancement of Science and Art" in New York City, wrote to her in January, 1920: "If you are not engaged will you come to the Woman's Art School at Cooper Union next Wednesday afternoon and let the class in modeling see your figure—we should be glad if you could give us a four weeks' pose from 1-4 pm."

ULRIC H. ELLERHUSEN

The architectural sculptor Ulric H. Ellerhusen studied at the Art Institute of Chicago under Karl Bitter and at the Art Student League in New York. His works include the *Oregon Pioneer* atop the Oregon State Capitol Dome, and the Rockefeller Chapel of the University of Chicago, with more than fifty statues to his credit including the noteworthy *March of Religion* spanning the front gable.

Some of his crowning achievements could be seen at the Panama-Pacific International Exposition in 1915, for which he created, at the Palace of Fine Arts, the *Weeping Woman* on the colonnade flower box, decorations on the massive flower receptacles, and the figural sculptures between painted panels.

Ellerhusen wrote to Princess White Deer on November 21, 1920, in care of the Globe Theatre, while she was performing in the musical *Tip Top*. He said:

> I'm about to complete, with three other heads representing the four principal races of man, an ideal portrait of Pocahontas, as representing America.
>
> In the conception of this head I have been using your pictures to some extent and Mr. Ivory thought it likely that you would consent to give me enough of your time so that I could at least compare your head with my clay model before it was cast in plaster. At the same time I would also like to have the benefit of your authentic knowledge of the subject.
>
> These heads will be erected and unveiled nexst <sic> spring in Elmwood Park, East Orange, N.J., and Mrs. Woodrow Wilson, being a descendant of Pocahontas, is expected to be present. The matter will receive publicity then, of course, but I believe that in the meantime your publicity man would consider the fact of your

CHAPTER FIVE: ARTISTS AND SCHOLARS • 145

Princess White Deer, photographed by Alfred Cheney Johnston for the Ziegfeld Follies.

having co-laborated with me on this work as quite useful for his purposes.

The statue she would pose for would be called *The Peace Monument*. Originally it was to be named *The Shrine of Human Rights* and was proposed by the son of Joel Francis Freeman, who donated $150,000 for the beautification of a park in honor of the memory of his father. Elmwood Park, located in East Orange, New Jersey, was a former ash dump turned into a children's park.

The envisioned sculptural group was four pedestals, seven feet in height, supporting four figures of eight feet in height. Each figure was a bust, modeled to represent Confucius, Columbus, Pocahontas, and Frederick Douglas, who represented Asia, Europe, America, and Africa. Mrs. Woodrow Wilson, a descendent of Pocahontas, did indeed come to its dedication.

Sometime during the construction of the Garden State Parkway in 1954, three of the statues along with the torch and shrine were removed. Their location remains unknown, and only Confucius remains.

ALFRED CHANEY JOHNSTON

Alfred Chaney Johnston was the official photographer for Florenz Ziegfeld, Jr.'s *Follies* from 1917 to 1931. His photographs were considered risqué in their time, but are mild by today's standards. Johnston was known for his tapestry backgrounds and props of shawls, strands of pearls, and the sheerest of flimsy scarves. He photographed more than 25,000 beauties in his studio and lived lavishly at the Hotel des Artistes. Princess White Deer posed for him in costume upon her blanket.

E. O. HOPPÉ

In 1921, at the age of thirty, Esther posed for the renowned portraitist E. O. (Emil Otto) Hoppé. One of his photographs of her was chosen for his *Book of Fair Women* in 1922, a remarkable series of celebrated women. The book was published in a limited number of 560 hand-numbered editions. An article by John O'Donnell made its way across the United States through California, Utah, Wisconsin, Indiana, and Virginia under such similar titles as "Beauty Expert Picks World's Beauties," "Picks World's Most Beautiful Women," and "Picks World's Beauties," publicizing Hoppé's international beauty expertise and his forthcoming book of 32 beauties.

Princess White Deer, photographed by E. O. Hoppé as one of the world's most beautiful women and included in his Book of Fair Women.

Sally James Farnham, the sculptress of Central Park's famous Simón Bólivar statue and of the tombstone of Irene and Vernon Castle entitled *At the end of the Day* at Woodlawn Cemetery, said that her choice of beauty is the agile type of woman that "Princess White Deer, Indian dancer, comes closest in her estimation of feminine loveliness... She is about five feet five, beautifully proportioned with lithe, muscular figure that to me is marvelous."

ALEXANDER STIRLING CALDER

The American sculptor Alexander Stirling Calder was both the son of and the father of a sculptor. He attended the Pennsylvania Academy of Fine Arts, the Academie Julian, and École des Beaux-Arts in Paris before returning home to Philadelphia, where he is known for the Swann Memorial Fountain, the Shakespeare Memorial, and the gateposts and fountain at the University Museum.

Calder and Karl Bitter were named heads of the Sculptural Program for the Panama-Pacific Exposition in San Francisco. It is Calder's *The Nations of the West* that sits atop the Arch of the Setting Sun.

Calder wrote to Esther on February 28, 1922:

> Dear Miss White Deer:
> Some years ago you were brought to see me at my old studio at 51 W. 10th St. I would now like to see you with a view to posing for a statue that I wish to make and would be glad to have you telephone or call if you receive this. In case you are not in New York, could you tell me of any other Indian girl who poses?
> Yours truly,
> A. Stirling Calder

More of Calder's works can be seen in one of New York City's designated historic landmark buildings located at Broadway at 46th. The building was commissioned by I. Miller, who specialized in selling beautiful footwear to Broadway dancers and actors, and who wanted statues in the niches of women in the arts. Calder carved the stone figures of Ethel Barrymore who represented drama; Marilyn Miller, musical comedy; Rose Ponselle, opera; and Mary Pickford, motion pictures. Another of his works is *George Washington,* is one of the two freestanding statues flanking the Washington Square Arch.

PARAMOUNT PICTURES

Princess White Deer received a letter on May 27, 1925, from Famous Players-Lasky Corporation, better known as Paramount Pictures, from their offices on Fifth Avenue in New York City.

> Dear Madame:
> At your convenience will you please come in to see Mr. Walter Wanger. He would like to have a little chat with you in connection with the possibility of your doing a picture for us.

Whether or not they ever had their little chat is unrecorded; and if they did, whatever they spoke of remains unknown.

CURT E. ENGELBRECHT

Trained in Germany, Curt E. Engelbrecht came to the United States in 1912 to learn American news photography. He later worked for the *New York Times* and Motion Picture–Fox News; of note were his films of the Graf Zeppelin at various takeoffs and landings, and the Bremen flyers. A highlight of his career and a feather in his cap was the first and only filming of John D. Rockefeller, on his 90th birthday.

In June of 1930, a year after he had spent his summer vacationing in Lake Mohawk, Engelbrecht joined the community's publication, *The Papoose,* in the capacity of public relations, and provided "two bucks" to keep *The Papoose* going. His photo lab and office were set up in the Lake Mohawk Blacksmith Shop next to the Riding Academy at the end of the boardwalk. For 35 years he memorialized in photography the events and people that made up the community's history. His talent captured Princess White Deer in all her beauty in crisp detail in 1932 and 1937. It is his portrait of her that hangs in the Country Club.

MUSIC

Seventy-five years after Esther posed for the *Book of Fair Women*, the grandson of E. O. Hoppé, keyboardist Michael Hoppé, along with the alto flutist Tim Wheaton, composed and performed *The Yearning: Romances for Alto Flute*, and released it in 1996.

The artists describe the piece as "Romances…lyrical compositions suggestive of passionate love songs whose qualities are ones of tenderness, intimacy and yearning. Each Romance is individually dedicated to the celebrated women featured in a remarkable series of photographs by the renowned photographer E. O. Hoppé (1878–1972)." The romance entitled Indigo Sunset was dedicated to Princess White Deer. This composition is a hauntingly beautiful melody that conjures the spirit of a peaceful forest whose voice is as soft as a mist.

The photograph accompanying the piece is not the same as from *Fair Women* but another entirely. Interestingly, in this E. O. Hoppé photograph Esther is dressed in the exact same costume as the one she wore in *Ziegfeld Follies* and when photograph by Alfred Cheney Johnston. The blanket wrapped about her waist is the same one that she sat on in the previous photo; the bodice of the costume, hair ornaments, and arm band are the same. The style of the two photographers with the exact same subject matter couldn't be more artistically different, and each is beautifully captured.

THE COLOR OF COSTUMES

The blanket of the Hoppé and Johnston photographs still survives, and the colors are vibrant. The background is a rich, saturated red flecked with small white geometric specks. Dominating the center of the blanket is a geometric motif in alternating shades of flaming orange and red and outlined in bold yellow. The blanket is edged in variegated stripes of white, green, purple, and red of different widths.

It is difficult to imagine the actual colors of her costumes because photography had only advanced to black and white development. Thankfully her family has lovingly preserved and tenderly stored costumes such as James Deer's suede tunic of tobacco brown with fringe, which was worn with a roomy tunic shirt of bright red; and Esther's beaded dance moccasins of red and blue patterns on white bead background, plus the hand-beaded bands of trim that covered her costumes.

Esther's full-feathered performance bonnet is comprised of eagle feathers tipped with small red and purple feathers. Each quill is bound to the headdress with red wrappings and attached to an iridescent fawn-colored beaded headband. The center of the headband is a beadwork pyramid, with the center square beaded the same color as the background; the next step is an outline of ruby red followed by white, the deepest indigo blue, and ending with a last level of five steps of ruby red. A soft green beaded vine traces its way to each temple, where bonnet ribbons of black, red and sky-blue escape bulls eye medallions and would have draped over her shoulders.

Her blanket and her father's are of complementary colors of the deepest sienna, black, and white, plus the new green of spring, a deeper vegetable-plant green, the orange of clay or autumn leaves, the fiery red of maple leaves at their peak in autumn, and sunflower yellow. James Deer's blanket is a flame stitch pattern of row upon row of color; the center is a diamond

Princess White Deer photographed by E. O. Hoppé and featured on the packaging of the Michael Hoppé album that included his composition "Indigo Sunset," dedicated to her.

pattern in those colors forming herringbone angles. Its years of use show in signs of having been mended deeply in the center; the repaired tears still maintain their pattern despite the obvious sutures. Esther's blanket is bordered on each end with stripes of those same colors and a midsection of deepest sienna, with a centerpiece of nine diamond-shaped panes edged in green and white; six panes are a fleur-dis-lis shape, two flower panes are on a background of sunflower yellow, and four flower panes are on a background of white. The remaining three panes are bursts of colors forming motion: two are the hues of a setting sun, but the center pane starts out black and goes to a progressively lighter green with a yellow center.

THE SCHOLARS

Much has been written in scholarly works of Esther's Deer's performances as Princess White Deer. She is mentioned in anthropology textbooks, and she is named in the foundation of scholarly writing in the cited primary source on Mohawk entertainment and has been the subject of papers presented by doctorates.

In 1984, David Blanchard became a primary source for future studies when he wrote an article, "For Your Entertainment Pleasure—Princess White Deer and Chief Running Deer—Last 'Hereditary' Chief of the Mohawk: Northern Mohawk Rodeos and Showmanship," which was published in the *Journal of Canadian Culture*. Blanchard was the first to document the professional lives of the Deer Family. His paper is cited in no less than four university textbooks in subjects such as Social Sciences, Art, Native American Studies, and Canadian History.

The textbooks written by leading scholars are *Antimodernism and Artistic Experience: Policing the Boundaries of Modernity (2001)* by Lynda Jessup; *The Imaginary Indian: The Image of the Indian in Canadian Culture* (1992) by Daniel Francis; *Questions of Tradition* (2004) by Gordon J. Schochet and Mark Phillips; *Unpacking Culture: Art and Commodity in Colonial and Postcolonial Worlds* (1999) by Ruth Bliss Phillips and Christopher Burghard Steiner; *Royal Spectacle: The 1860 Visit of the Prince of Wales to Canada and the United States* (2004) by Ian Walter Radforth; *Canadian Indian Cowboys in Australia: Representation, Rodeo* (2006) by Lynda Mannik.

Lynda Jessup's subject "antimodernism" can be described as

the international reaction to the onslaught of the modern world in the decades around the turn of the 20th century. Jessup's volume explores antimodernism as an artistic response.

The work of Ruth Bliss Phillips, *Performing the Native Woman: Primitivism and Mimicry in Early Twentieth–Century Visual Culture*, was referenced in Jessup's works, and Phillips' *Disappearing Acts: Tradition of Exposure, Traditions of Enclosure and Iroquois Masks* was included in *Question of Tradition* by Schochet and (Mark) Phillips.

Ruth Bliss Phillips, who holds a Canadian research chair and is Professor of Art History at Carleton University, Ottawa, partnered with Trudy Nicks to present a paper to the American Indian Workshop, *From Wigwam to White Lights: Princess White Deer's Indian Acts,* in Oporto, Portugal, in 1995. Trudy Nicks is with Royal Ontario Museum and the Department of Anthropology at McMaster University. She has presented *From Wigwam to White Lights* as recently as March 2007 at the Anthropology Speaker Series at McMaster University. Ruth Bliss Phillips has extensive research published in the fields of Native American Art and Native American Women. Together Nicks and Phillips believed that "By selectively appropriating aspects of modernist primitives, White Deer's re-enactments countered the dominant notion of the Vanishing Indian and insist on the modernity of indigenous people."

Princess White Deer is mentioned in no fewer than ten books on the subjects of Broadway, Theater, and Cole Porter.

The *Best Plays* series, highlighting the best of American drama, were published each yearby Burns Mantle and Louis Kronenberger. The Broadway plays Esther performed in were noted in the years 1919–1920, 1921, 1923, and 1927.

Her performances on Broadway are also noted in *The Blue Book of Broadway Musicals, Revue: A Nostalgic Reprise of the Great Broadway Period* (1962); *The Dial* (1918); *American Musi-*

cal Theatre: A Chronicle; The Billboard Yearbook of the New York Legitimate Stage (1932); The Best Plays of 1919 to 1920 and the Year Book of the Drama in America (2005); A Chronology of American Musical Theater (1978, 1986, and 1992); William Carlos Williams: A New World Naked (1990); The Life that Late He Led: A Biography of Cole Porter (1967); and American Songwriters: An H. W. Wilson Biographical Dictionary (1967).

THE NATURE OF SYNCOPATION

In the world of musical studies, Columbia University Professor William Patterson, Ph.D., investigated the individual difference in the sense of rhythm of jazz, returning to its roots in the African jungle. His is an interesting early theory with unveiled racist references to savages, written at a time when such attitudes were, in parts of the country, considered standards of decency and appropriateness. Professor Patterson argued that modern society has inhibited many native/natural instincts in us by keeping a conventional dignity which forbids body-swaying or toe-tapping to music that gives us pleasure. Society's sophistication has "deprived us of unsuspected pleasures."

In an article that posed the question "Who invented Jazz?", Ken-tio-kwi-osta, (Princess White Deer's Indian name) said "the redskins." She insisted that "it was her people who, with their tom-toms, originated splitting beats to infinitesimals, which is the essence of syncopation." She worked with Professor Patterson at Columbia University "in his elaborate laboratory experiments upon the nature of syncopation."

In another article, Princess White Deer discussed how she and Paul Whiteman, whom she knew from when they performed together in *Lucky* in 1927, discussed Indian music and how he would take down her melodies and utilize them in his orchestra.

Whiteman had sensed the transition of popular music from ragtime to jazz, and organized a dance band in San Francisco in 1918. Later he moved to New Jersey, before settling in New York in 1920, where he became the best-known American bandleader. His lush orchestral style was widely copied on countless bandstands at home and abroad.

Whiteman was one of the most important figures in 20th century American pop music. Formed at a time when the country's musical landscape was changing, Whiteman's orchestra broke much new ground. His was the first orchestra to popularize arrangements, the first to use full reed and brass sections, the first to play in vaudeville, the first to travel to Europe, the first to use a female singer (Mildred Bailey), and the first to use a vocal trio. Whiteman's greatest legacy to jazz lies in his eye for talent. His alumni include such luminaries as Bailey, Jimmy Dorsey, Tommy Dorsey, Bing Crosby, and Johnny Mercer.

PBS

Esther was featured in the PBS series, *A Year of Women: Women in Arts & Entertainment*. A lesson page—*A Year of Women, Lost in History* for student studies—was web-designed for educators, covering teaching points, discussion points, and activity extensions.

Discussion points included the Akwesasne Reservation, minority women in the theater, the *Follies* and Wild West shows, and the concept of an Ambassador of the Mohawk People. Activity extensions suggested researching the New Jersey community and visiting the Akwesasne Museum and Cultural Center in Hogansburg, New York.

THE SMITHSONIAN NATIONAL MUSEUM OF THE AMERICAN INDIAN

In 2002 an Exhibit entitled *Across Borders: Beadwork in Iroquois Life* was displayed at the George Gustav Heye Center of the Smithsonian National Museum of the American Indian, located in lower Manhattan; and was organized by the McCord Museum of Montreal and the Castellani Art Museum of Niagara University, along with the Kanien'kehaka Raotitiohkwa Cultural Center of the Kahnawake reservation. More than 300 items of Iroquois beadwork traveled with the exhibit including items made for the tourist trade. Beads adorned all manner of Indian outfits, "but a particularly fetching one," wrote Grace Glueck for the *New York Times*,

> ... is the deerskin ensemble worn by one of the most best-known Mohawk entertainers, Princess White Deer, nee Esther Deer. A member of a family enterprise, "The Famous Deer Brothers Champion Indian Trick Riders of the World," which performed across Europe and America in the early 1900's, she became an acclaimed singer and dancer in American vaudeville shows. Her playful costume, from about 1910 to 1920, consisted of a beaded deerskin bikini, a bra top, a headdress and boots with beaded cuffs. The beaded symbols include several swastikas; an ancient motif used by aboriginal artists and thought to represent the sun and the cycle of time, predating by millenniums the adoption of the sign by the Nazi Party. As a whole the outfit is strictly Mohawk-Hollywood.

CHAPTER SIX
Life Beyond the Footlights

THE PERSONAL SIDE

Of all the articles written about Princess White Deer, the one that was most personally revealing appeared in *Gouverneur Free Press* on Wednesday, June 22, 1927, in an article on page two entitled "Real Princess Returns to Old Reservation. White Deer, who has won fame on Stage, a Direct Descendent of Last Hereditary Chief of St. Regis Mohawks."

The unnamed reporter, who didn't have a byline, seemed to have been entranced by his subject to the point of falling in love with her. He wrote a very complimentary article.

The interview revealed that Esther had spent her childhood on the St. Regis and Caughnawaga Reservations. Several years of her life were spent in a tiny cabin with her parents near Hogansburg. Her early education was in a school on the reservation and at the Caughnawaga School, but it was interrupted when her father and Uncle John formed a show troupe called the Deer Brothers, which originated the first Indian trick-riding show, and took the family with them to Europe. This troupe performed with larger Wild West shows.

Princess White Deer revealed to the reporter that she learned dancing and riding early and received her theatrical training from Indian showmen. Her first American manager was William Morris of Saranac Lake and her present manager was Sir Harry Lauder. Her upcoming venture was now in vaudeville with Keith, her act entitled *From Wigwam to White Lights,* and she had recently met popularity as a singer in her one-hour radio program, *American Indian Idyll.*

The reporter described Esther as "strikingly beautiful" and compared her to fantasy "calendar pictures of Indian beauties, the type almost never seen in real life." She was educated, with refined poise and perfect manners, and dressed with "exceptionally good taste" in the height of style. She was slim and "lithe as a boy." She lived in an apartment in New York City and had a country home at an undisclosed location on the Hudson (which in actuality was the home in Port Chester that her father called White Deer Lodge). She painted and sculpted some.

She was an active woman, enjoyed all outdoor sports, and particularly liked to swim, shoot, skate, and play lacrosse and tennis. She was a golf enthusiast with ambition to be competent in the sport. She had recently taken up of polo, which came naturally to her, as she was an expert horsewoman, having ridden since her childhood. She loved dogs and horses.

What he didn't know was that she rose at the "crack of noon" every day. Even after she retired, she kept those hours. She was a voracious reader and read deep into the night. She loved bacon for breakfast. She wasn't much of a cook and neither was her cousin May. Esther would give it a try from time to time, but she had a tendency to overcook everything.

May's daughter Sylvia learned the basics of cooking at school from the Sisters of St. Anne, and the fine art of Indian cookery by watching her aunt Josephine. Because her mother and Esther were *Ziegfeld Follies* girls on Broadway, they weren't much given to the domestic arts.

Esther liked new cars and was often photographed with them in the near background, along with family and friends.

Recognized wherever she traveled, even when she didn't travel under her stage name, Esther took to protecting her privacy by often misstating her address. When asked to provide personal information that would be recorded on a ship's manifest, instead of giving her true address at the Plaza Annex she would give the address as 69th Street. For the unknowing purser it sounded like a true address; but a New Yorker would know the location was in the middle of Central Park. Little twists of facts didn't seem to bother her, for both she and her mother seldom stated their true age, and at times neither did her father. These little deceptions were recorded on official documents, including Esther's birth certificate, in which both Georgette and James had adjusted their ages. On the fourteenth Census of the United States, taken in 1920 for Tonawanda City, Erie County, New York, Jim did accurately give his age as 54, but his wife and daughter shaved off a few years. Georgette stated she was 46, when in fact she was 49, and Esther said she was 23 when in fact she was 29.

She was a partner in two businesses: one was a drug store and cosmetic counter concession, the other a night club in Harlem, New York. Their names are lost to anyone's memory, and Esther did not save any record of them. Whenever she traveled north to visit, she never forgot to bring May and the children gifts of perfumes and powders. The toiletries delighted the little girls.

Esther had a magical childhood as a traveling Mohawk. She grew up in a loving home with her father's immediate family around her. Her mother Georgette loved her father James to the point of adoration, as he loved her.

Esther did not have a formal education; her traditional schooling was sporadic. She recalled a first grade teacher, Miss Anna Kreitner in Buffalo School No. 5, but mostly her education was attended to by Georgette and James at home, or on the road. She did not lack, for she had the skills, talents and abilities of any highly educated young lady coming from a regarded university or college. It was noted in two newspapers that they thought she was a graduate of Vassar.

Esther loved to laugh, loved a good joke, and was rarely angry—the rare occurrence was usually regarding her career, for she was most precise about her work and expected perfection.

ROMANCE—REAL, IMAGINED, AND STILL TALKED ABOUT

No one from North America ever met or knew Count Joseph Alex Krasicki. His and Esther's romance and marriage had happened far from home in Russia and ended shortly thereafter with his death in World War I, after Esther's return home to the United States. Stories such as this prevailed in those days and were not much talked about as they conjured up thoughts of sadness and loss.

She was escorted to important events by the most handsome of her contemporaries; she did not lack for male companionship and she received many marriage proposals during her life... none of which was accepted.

YOUNG LOVE

As young as 13, while traveling between Johannesburg and Pretoria with Texas Jack's Wild West Show, Esther captured the heart of a young man who presented her with a token of his affection. He is identified only as "J. R." on the silver charm. The two medallions, similar to arcade tokens or dog tags where messages could be engraved quickly, were given to her from each city.

THE FARMER'S SON

In November 1919, the *New York Times*' "The Playgoer" wrote:

> If Princess White Deer had married the young Indian blood of her father's choice she would probably be milking the cows and bringing up a large family on

a farm on the St. Regis reservation near Malone, New York, instead of shaking a wicked shimmy in "Hitchy-Koo 1919" at the Liberty Theatre. For while Princess White Deer is of royal Indian blood her father and grandfather before him were simple farmers on the Government reservation where the last of the Iroquois are now living.

It was the ambition of Mr. Running Deer, the father of Princess White Deer, to have her marry the son of Mr. Red Bull, who lives on the adjoining farm, and in that way enlarge the Deer estates. But Princess White Deer decided differently. Just days before the day set for the marriage she came to New York.

Whether this was written tongue in cheek is hard to determine. The hype of leaving a groom behind in Malone, New York, to perform on the stage was nothing more than media fabrication attaching a little mystery to a cast member. Raymond Hitchcock went on to tell "The Playgoer" that he had seen Princess White Deer dancing on the roof of the New Amsterdam Theatre in *Ziegfeld Midnight Frolic* and engaged her for *Hitchy-Koo*—the interview in which he said "she does the shimmy 'pretty'" and "An Indian Princess gives my support a strange wild flavor."

It was not in least likely that this story was true. Chief Running Deer had a long theatrical career and trained his own children to perform. The chances are slim to none that her grandfather and father did any farming. Chances are slimmer yet that he would wish that his only grandchild, who had been performing with the family since the age of four in Wild West Shows, who had beauty, talent, and promise be nothing more than a farmer's wife and mother of a large brood of children. Esther never lived on the reservation. Bits of the story were true: She did perform in Germany and Russia at music halls over a two year contract. She did stay in St. Petersburg (Petrograd), Russia. The phrase "settled down in Petrograd" implies her brief married life, and she did return to the United States at the beginning of the Russian revolution. She did perform on the roof of the New Amsterdam with the *Ziegfeld Midnight Frolic*. She did model for Penhryn Stanlaws and Harrison Fisher.

A BOY FROM BACK HOME

But there was a boy, a boy from back home where her grandfather lived, who carried the torch for Esther. Among Esther's mementos is his image captured in a photograph on a winter day outside the old International Hotel on St. Regis. He is the man sitting behind the reins of a horse-drawn sleigh who looks happily out at the camera despite the coldness of the day. He

A boy from back home. Chief Running Deer and John Jacco in a sleigh outside of the International Hotel on the St. Regis reservation.

and the man sitting beside him are wearing bearskin coats, and a bearskin carriage blanket lies across their laps. The old International Hotel on St. Regis fills the background behind them.

He drove from Caughnawaga to Hogansburg each time Esther came to visit in winter. He was her ardent admirer. With each visit, a dance was held in her honor. Each time he drove out to see her, John Jacco asked Esther to marry him. It was the talk of the town, fodder for small-town gossip, fueled each winter at the dance to which everyone was invited and the young, dashing John attended. Later, when John was resigned to the fact that Esther would not marry him and he married another, that small-town gossip would cause John's wife and her sister to shun Esther in an attempt to maintain her wifely dignity—as the town recognized that her personality paled when compared to Esther's vivaciousness and everyone could tell that a part of John still belonged to her.

THE RACE CAR DRIVER

On the road with *Hitchy-Koo* in California, Esther met a man while traveling on a train. His name is long forgotten by those who remember the story, all that remains is his occupation; he was a race car driver. From the first moment she saw him, she was drawn to him. Later he would tell her that he too was drawn to her the moment he saw her. It was love at first sight. It was the first time Esther had been drawn to another man since the death of her husband. He invited her to lunch with him on the train. The luncheon lengthened into cocktails and champagne. In that short period of time he professed his love for her but had to confess a truth: he was on his way to marry his fiancée. If she said the word he would end his engagement, cancel his wedding and marry her instead. She said no. After the trip, he sent a car to her hotel. Esther told him that this could not be, she couldn't be the cause of such unhappiness for another, that she, like him, had her obligations. She told him that her parents were like her own children and she must care for them as they had cared for her.

THE BANDLEADER

It was only after her liaison with Abe Lyman, the big-band orchestra leader and writer of such songs as "Mandalay," "Sweet Little You," and "You're In The Army Now," that their relationship came to light in an article entitled "They Love Abe's Love-Songs BUT" that appeared in *The Port Arthur News* on February 9, 1936, with pictures of six of his paramours.

Abe Lyman began as a Chicago taxi driver before he made it in Hollywood by obtaining the coveted position of leader at the Cocoanut Grove at the Ambassador Hotel in Los Angeles—the famous nightclub spot of jazz musicians and gorgeous women. He was handsome, personable, and had an athletic physique and a winning smile. His career soared, capturing the attention of Charlie Chaplin with whom with he composed "Sing A Song" and "With You, Dear, In Bombay" in 1925. His band, Abe Lyman's California Orchestra, appeared in Chaplin's movie, *The Gold Rush*, with Chaplin playing the role of conductor. Abe and his orchestra recorded many songs with the Brunswick label until 1936, and later for Decca and Bluebird, the RCA Victor label. The Abe Lyman orchestra played engagements in New York City and Atlantic City, traveled to Europe and appeared at the Kit Cat Club and Palladium in London, and at the Moulin Rouge and Perroquet in Paris. In the 1930s his orchestra appeared in Warner Brothers films, and he recorded the opening for the black and white *Merrie Melodies* cartoons. Abe and his orchestra appeared in 10 movies and many short "talkies." He had moved to New York by 1933, and he led his orchestra in two radio network series, *Waltz Time* in 1933 and *Your Hit Parade* in 1937. He left the music industry around the age of 50 and went into the restaurant business. He died in 1957 at the age of 60.

The full-page article paraded out all the loves in Abe Lyman's life, starting with Thelma Todd, the comedienne and screen actress who appeared with the Marx Brothers and other comedy greats, to whom he was engaged during his Hollywood days until she eloped with the movie agent Pat Ciaco; and following with all the equally beautiful and talented women the charismatic bandleader wooed and lost, including Princess White Deer.

Abe had met Princess White Deer in one of New York City's nightclubs. She is described as regal and slender with long black braids and black eyes as deep as the pools her forefathers drank from; but she had a tempestuous and possessive spirit, the journalist wrote in his not very witty, not very clever attempt at amusing the reader, claiming this was due to "those wild and possessive forefathers," unwittingly promoting false ethnic stereotyping. Princess White Deer and Abe Lyman fought about his popularity with the women who adored his music, and the relationship floundered. The journalist further embellished his story by comparing Abe to a modern brave "who swung a baton instead of a tomahawk and discovered that his love songs didn't have enough to 'charm to soothe the savage breast.'"

After Esther, Abe Lyman had been engaged to an opera singer who, after sending hot telegrams to her "precious" that were known to "burn up the wires" during their telephone-telegraph courtship, dumped him for a constable of the Northwest Mounted Police in Montreal. Then came a tap dancer who pursued her own career as soon as Abe was on the road; and yet another who "calmly left for England at the height of Abe's torchy wooing."

Abe Lyman may have been charming and attractive, with a voice so sweet that women swooned while listening to him; but despite the packaging, women left him perhaps because he was always plying his charms and looking for his next conquest. None of the women involved with Abe Lyman ever gave him a backward glance. Even though Princess White Deer was listed as one of his many paramours, her virtue of preferring a monogamous relationship stands out from the rest of the women. Although she never talked about her relationship with Abe, she did save all his letters to her and kept them among the treasures of her life.

NATIVE AMERICAN ACTIVISM, PATRIOTISM, CIVIC AND SOCIAL ACTIVITIES

Early in Esther's career she took advantage of her popularity as Princess White Deer to promote Native American causes, knowing her name would generate newspaper articles—as evidenced in 1917 when she had promoted patriotism and Liberty Bonds. In 1918, "Fails to Fool Indian Princess" was reported. As a guest of Camp Wadsworth in Spartanburg, South Carolina, she proved her keenness of eye in detecting the soldiers' movements during camouflage training.

1921 brought changes in her publicity when she appeared before a United States Press Conference to promote the native issues of the Vote for Women and Red Faction in the next presidential election.

Articles appeared with titles such as "On Warpath for Votes for Americans"; "Votes for Squaws is Battle Cry of Mohawk Indians"; "Indian Princess to Fight for Ballot"; "Princess White Deer Wants Votes For Squaws"; "New Susan B. Anthony Takes Up Tomahawk To Win Votes For Squaws"; and the report that Esther "declared that there would be a real red faction at the next Presidential election, if the hopes of squaws are fulfilled" appeared across the northern Midwest and Western United States, with the *Modesto Evening News* carrying it on the front page, above the fold.

In the interview she gave to *United Press* correspondent Paul Malone, she said, "The only impediment that hangs between the Squaw and the ballot box is fear of heavy taxation.". . . "The Indian could have obtained that privilege could have been obtained long ago if not for fear of losing his land, all he has left." She believed it was the Indian woman who will salvage the bulk of redskin misfortune and win the voting right…the appointment of an Indian Commissioner in Washington, D.C., was the first step.

Esther attended all Native American functions she was invited to, whether to perform or to attend for pleasure. She was honored to be invited to two Six Nations events, and to society functions that benefited Native Americans.

In February of 1925, she attended the Aztec Ball, and later that summer, on August 20, was invited to perform in an evening celebration marking a historic day of ceremonies to install 18 Oneida Nation Chiefs as part of the final steps in the rehabilitation of the Six Nations, conducted by the Chiefs in the grove at Oneida's natural amphitheatre. A few years later, in 1928, *The Syracuse Herald* reported that she was again a featured dancer at the Six Nation's event in Central New York.

Princess White Deer told the *Galveston Daily News*, in a 1927 articled entitled "An Indian Revue," that she had made exhaustive studies of the red man's influence upon art, music, dancing, and costume in the theater, with a view of staging an elaborate Indian revue. The Indian Bureau of the Department of the Interior gave aid in her research and she finally accumulated so much material that a book was the result. The story was repeated on May 11, 1927, in the *Warren Tribune* of Warren, Pennsylvania. Unfortunately no copy of her manuscript can be located.

At an assembly of 200 Native Americans drawn together to observe the Annual Indian Day in Prospect Park in Queens, New York, the agenda of the Conclave of September 1929 was to plead for solidarity to preserve the identity of the Indian race—a plea that the *Brooklyn Daily Eagle* reported was half-heartedly agreed to. Princess White Deer and her father, James Deer, were among the noteworthy native men and women who had come from across the nation to support the plea for solidarity, including Chief Yellow Robe of the Rosebud Agency of the Sioux tribe, one of the first of 18 enrolled at the Carlisle Indian School; the author Buffalo Child Long Lance; Red Wind of the song that bears her name; Hermkaw White Wing of the Winnebago; Princess Watawaso of the Penobscott; and Princess Spotted Elk and her sister Darly Little Elk, also of the Penobscott tribe and currently with the cast of *Fiesta*.

The *Brooklyn Daily Eagle* noted that of the 250 Indians who lived in New York City, 200 resided in Brooklyn and were employed in trades such as iron and steel, building, acting, medicine shows, professional jobs, and sailing.

On October 23, 1929, *The Brooklyn Daily Eagle* ran a picture of James Deer in a spectacular war bonnet and reported that Mohawk Chief Running Deer would take part in the ceremonies of the unveiling of three tablets commemorating the Battle of Long Island. The day-long celebration commenced in the morning with the unveiling ceremonies at three locations: the site of Livingston Mansion, home of Declaration of Independence signer Philip Livingston at Joralemon Street and Sidney Place; Four Chimneys, Washington's headquarters at the head of Montague Street; and Ferry Landing at the foot of Fulton Street, where the American Army embarked during its retreat. This was followed by a reception at Borough Hall and a parade at 2:30 p.m. starting at Prospect Park Plaza. The Columbus Club on Prospect Park West hosted the luncheon, and a Colonial tea from 4:00 to 6:00 p.m. was hosted by the Long Island Federation of Women's Clubs at Plymouth Church on Orange Street. The day's closing event was a banquet at 8:00 p.m. at Leverich Tower Hotel.

James Deer had accepted James S. Graham's invitation the Washington commemorative exercises and agreed to don the "official regalia of his office" to "typify the original American in the pageant."

In 1932 Esther performed in *The Coming of Pa'Yatamu* at

the John Golden Theatre for the Indian Benefit of the Society of First Sons and Daughters of America, with Chief Yowlache, the famous basso of Yakima, Washington.

On August 8, 1933, *The Daily Item* of Port Chester, New York reported that on September 27 Port Chester resident Chief Deer would enact the role of Quarropas at the 250th anniversary of the purchase of White Plains from the Indians. Quarropas was the chieftain from whom the early settlers of Rye purchased the land on which the county seat was built. Chief Deer took the opportunity to promote a picture of himself with his daughter.

In September, Princess White Deer became a nominee for "Who is the Greatest Indian of Today" based on her ability as a Mohawk interpreter of classical dances and her Broadway stardom.

Living in Yonkers, New York, in 1935, James Deer appeared in the first of ceremonies to honor the city's Tercentenary Anniversary over the next four years, leading up to the countywide celebration on August 3, 1939. The event was billed as a colorful ceremony on a Saturday night at the Hudson River Boat Club Pier.

Chief Deer, who lived at 4 Midland Avenue at that time, directed a program of songs of the red man, peace pipe ceremonies, lament chants, folk melodies, and dances of victory and greeting on the pier at the foot of Ashton Road. Cherokee, Algonquin, and Mohawk told stories of the great hunts and the wondrous days when Indians ruled this land. Indian entertainers of the Algonquin included Chief Dan Red Eagle and Princess White Fawn; and of the Mohawk, Frances Chickadee, Chief Lone Pine, and Chief Deer's niece, Leah Deer, who performed in tribal costume. Princess White Deer was expected to join her father in the pageantry.

Esther attended many Native American social balls with her father in 1934. When the Confederated Indian Tribes of America extended its cordial invitation to Esther, she and her father attended its Grand Pageant and Dance held at the Innisfail Ballroom at East 56th Street in New York on February 23, 1934.

Thirty-seven tribes of Indians in war paint, war bonnets, and native costumes entertained the guests with native songs and descriptive dances of their various tribes. General dancing followed until two o'clock with the orchestra directed by Chief Shunatona, Pawnee, who had been director of the world-famous U.S. Indian Band.

In May they attended the Indian Confederation of America costume ball at the George Washington Hotel in New York City. With tongue-in-cheek gaiety, Paul Harrison wrote of the evening in his column, "In New York," describing how the chiefs danced the double-lindy, maidens cavorted in the "Ziegfeldian" manner, and squaws wore evening gowns. The costume theme was to come dressed like palefaces.

Only entertainers and officials dressed in native regalia. Mr. Harrison noted the officials of the confederacy: Chief Shunatona as Sachem; Alexander Orchard, an official; Mrs. Owen, Keeper of Wampum; Leon Miller, Collector of Wampum; R. H. Johnson, Keeper of Records; and Max Major, Guard of Wigwam. The organization numbered 150 representing 50 tribes from as far north as Alaska and as far south as Central America.

He noted the lighthearted exchanges between him and the guests who taught him greetings and responses in Chippewa and Algonquin. He met Princess White Deer and her father, who gave him a lesson in "sign language."

Chief Shunatona and Princess White Deer would later perform at the Actors Dinner Club in the Hotel Woodstock on November 9, 1934.

1937—A VERY GOOD YEAR

It was a very good year for Chief James Deer. His energy was boundless; having just come off his Broadway production of

Russet Mantle, he attended powwows and Indian Day celebrations and worked on the July 5th powwow celebration, inviting dignitaries worldwide. His daughter was an active participant in his endeavors.

RUSSET MANTLE

Chief James Deer was hand-chosen to play the leading role in *Russet Mantle* by the producers, Jerome Mayer and Murray Jay Queen, after they searched for weeks to find an authentic Indian actor to play the lead. He was 70 years old when took the part and considered "more than middle-aged," but he had such a genial temperament that the theater company threatened, happily, to adopt him as their mascot.

The play, set in Santa Fe, New Mexico, opened on January 16, 1936, at Theatre Masque in New York City and ran for 117 performances. It closed in April that year.

Chief James Deer was very familiar with Santa Fe, as his father Chief Running Deer spent a considerable amount of time there.

Lynn Riggs, the playwright, was the son of a cattleman and of Cherokee blood and had written 15 plays, mostly about Old Indian territory. *Green Grow the Lilacs* was rated one of the ten best plays of 1931. *Russet Mantle* was his first attempt at a more contemporary subject and was both an artistic and financial success. It was a satirical comedy concerning the difficulties faced by youths of the current generation.

Brooks Atkinson, the drama critic of the *New York Times*, wrote in his review, "It was gorgeously acted last evening at the Masque Theatre, where it ought to hang its hat for a long time. For this is a fragment of the comédie humaine—wise, fresh and incorrigibly ridiculous, and by all odds the best thing Mr. Riggs has done... The spirit is gay and the thinking is sane... It is a temptation to say that *Russet Mantle* is a priceless comedy, but that phrase might be misconstrued and sound like patronizing comment. Let us say merely that it is modest, light, sensible and funny. Pure comedy, in fact."

Time Magazine wrote that *Russet Mantle* "is supposed to concern itself chiefly with a couple of young New Dealers who sound off at length about changing the system, but by curtain time, have succeeded only in conceiving an illegitimate baby. However, this juvenile and somewhat embarrassing love affair is not the thing which makes *Russet Mantle* a notable addition to the Broadway season. Instead of standing around as the background for the youngsters, the older members of the cast steal the show for themselves... simply flabbergasted Broadway by revealing an unsuspected talent for Grade A comic characterization."

POLITICAL BLUNDER AND THE IROQUOIS CONFEDERACY

James Deer had attempted to revitalize the Iroquois Confederacy. The full Mohawk Counsel of Traditional Chiefs was surprised by this, as the Nation was well and thriving under its current leadership.

Invitations to attend the Grand Council of the Ancient Iroquois Confederacy on the St. Lawrence, at the St. Regis Reservation on July 5, 1937, were sent out by James D. Deer, Esq., Honorary Head Chief and Chief of the Mohawks, St. Regis Reservation, from his Beech Street address in Yonkers, New York, to the Presidents of the United States and Governor General of Canada; to prime ministers and their cabinets; to the ambassadors of Great Britain, France, Germany, Italy, Soviet Russia, and Japan; and to all the governors of the states and premiers of all the Canadian provinces. In addition, he invited heads of motion pictures studios, broadcasting companies, and publishing houses, plus officials from all branches of the military, the Boy Scouts, the Girls Scouts, and the Camp Fire Girls.

Princess White Deer with President Roosevelt's secretary, M. H. McIntyre, at the White House on June 28, 1937. She was hand-delivering an invitation to the President to attend the Grand Council of the Ancient Iroquois Confederacy.

In an interview he gave to the *Syracuse Herald* James was reported as saying that he invited the recently abdicated King Edward VIII of England and his wife Wallis Simpson. A photograph accompanied the article of James with his daughter sitting on the arm of his chair.

Every day the mail brought bad news; the letters of regret began arriving.

On June 28, 1937, the Secretary of War wrote, "Dear Mr. Deer... a previous engagement prevented me from attending such a historic ceremony." The Canadian Legation in Washington responded on June 29, 1937, pleading, "Sir ... while I am very sorry that I will not be able to be present at this meeting may I express the wish that every success will attend it." July 2 brought a letter from The White House. M. H. McIntyre, Secretary to the President, on his behalf wrote, "My Dear Mr. Deer, the President has asked me to tell you... He regrets exceedingly that his plans are such that it will not be possible for him to accept."

There was no response from the abdicated Edward and Wallis.

Mohawk reaction to James Deer and others like him for appearing "more Indian than the Indian" was strong. Not unlike the other performers who returned to both Akwesasne and Kahnawake, James had spent most of his life away from the reservation; he had lived in and around New York City and had a big home in Port Chester, New York. Forgotten was the fact in March of 1926, he represented his people in an action against the State of New York on behalf of the Six Nations, to recover land upon which the Aluminum Company of America plant at Massena stands that was claimed by the St. Regis tribe. The case was argued before Judge Frank Cooper in United States District Court.

It was his father, Running Deer, who had returned to St. Regis to run the old International Hotel after his years performing. No matter that the Deer Family visited often and for months on end; they did not live on the reservation. His daughter Esther was neither raised nor educated on the reservation. He had not participated in the struggles to overturn the Indian Act, nor supported cultural and educational developments on the reserve during the years that he was on the road performing. He was not a chief.

It did not bother the Mohawk that retired entertainers served as "guests of honor" sponsored by fraternal organizations such as the Kiwanis, the Rotary Club, and Moose International, nor that they appeared in costume and made honorary members of the tribe at events that would appear in the newspaper the next day. It did bother the Mohawk when these entertainers took themselves seriously and presented themselves to other governments as true representatives of the Mohawk Nation.

Nonetheless, the Chiefs of the Six Nations Iroquois held their event on July 5, 1937, at the St. Regis Reservation beginning at 2:00 p.m. Members from the Onondaga, Oneida, Seneca, Tuscarora, Cayuga and Mohawk were present.

"Indians Urge A Union for World Peace"–"Six Nation Iroquois In Conclave Monday at Hogansburg" the headlines read. The *Plattsburg Daily Press* reported a concise summary of the day's event.

It was a blazingly hot day; the crowd that had gathered was of St. Regis, Mohawk Indians, and whites. Literature and programs were distributed describing this as the first ceremonial event to be convened since the pre-Revolutionary days of the Grand Council of the Six Nations.

The opening ritual was spoken in Onondaga and words of welcome in English by Head Chief George E. Thomas. The address, "The Meaning of Great Peace," was presented by Chief William Cornelius. A solo of Indian hymns was sung by Harriet Green. The address, spoken in the Indian languages, was given by Chief Livingston Crouse.

A speech was given by Laura Cornelius Kellogg, executive secretary of the Six Nations of Seymour, Wisconsin, entitled "The Kayanerengo and the Konanshionni: Their Place in Politics."

Mrs. Kellogg stated that "the basic idea of the Iroquois banding together to prevent wars, made them the most powerful group in America. That the ultimate object of the present movement is to revive the Iroquois League until it eventually takes in all tribes." This was the background and theme of her address.

In his speech, the peace advocate Charles Davis of England said that "it was not until he had formulated his plans did he learn that it was almost an exact duplicate of the constitution adopted by the Five Nations in 1570."

Several large silken flags were displayed at both sides of the platform. Davis referred to these in his speech. One was a replica of the flag that George Washington raised on January 2, 1776; another bore a British Union Jack in the corner and the 13 states represented in the stripes; and yet another was the Betsy Ross flag.

A new flag was proposed by Davis that contained the old continental flag, with an eight-point gold star in the center of the Union Jack to symbolize the union of English-speaking people and promote world peace.

Onondaga Chief George E. Thomas was master of ceremonies and introduced several visiting chiefs. "James Deer, one of the noted St. Regis tribesmen, had collapsed from the heat but was revived sufficiently to speak as scheduled. He strode out on the platform along with two venerable Indians in full feathered regalia."

Later Princess White Deer joined the platform. The traditional costume she wore was noted by the newspaper as a sharp contrast to heavy-handed use of lipstick and mascara, juxtaposing the old and the new.

The induction into honorary chiefhood of Charles Henry Davis was a colorful spectacle, making Davis a member of the Iroquois under the name "Safe Keeper of the Council Fire" in the Snipe Clan. Chief Deer took out the peace pipe, and each puffed and passed it to the next man. After this, a colorfully bold blanket was placed around Davis' shoulders. Davis, an elderly man, sweated profusely beneath the woolen blanket in the 120-degree heat.

Princess White Deer sang an Indian song, and a woman named Running Deer gave an original blanket dance. The gathering was partly adjourned when Chief Deer again stepped up to the microphone and began talking to the remaining audience of how he helped conquer the Nile with Wolseley at Khartoum.

Setbacks and disappointments didn't deter James Deer, as he still appeared at civic events that in any way honored Native Americans. On August 25, he spoke to the Kiwanis Club about his expedition up the Nile and the highlights of his life in Freeport, New York. The reality of what had transpired did take its toll on him and his health declined.

INDIANS BID FOR MANHATTAN

An auction opened the festivities of the Autumn Pow-Wow of Indian Confederation of America held on November 20 in New York.

Chief Clear Sky walked up to the microphone. His opening line to the audience: "They would bid thirty dollars for the Island of Manhattan." He pointed out to the head delegates of the Oneida, Hopi, Seneca, Chippewa, and Mohawk that their ancestors sold the island to the palefaces for twenty-four dollars, the extra six dollars was an allowance for the improvements they made.

The ballroom cheered and drums rolled. The crowd was silenced only when Chief James Deer of the Mohawks stood up at his ringside table, regal in his majestic war bonnet. He spoke: "I'll have a scotch and soda."

The rest of the evening was devoted to dancing, and so it was reported that the bid for Manhattan was the only business transaction. The celebrity-spotting of Molly Spotted Elk, a Penobscot, was mentioned as she took off her moccasins and did a corn dance to a tom-tom beat, described as the Indian equivalent of the Charleston.

A $50 prize was offered to the best dancer, who would be allowed to participate in the Indian international dance competition in which all nations competed. The Winnegos were led by Chief Blow Snake in a snake dance; the Chickahominy were led by Bright Eyes in a squaw dance; the Mohawk were led into a victory dance by Little Buffalo; and Good Eagle of the Winnebagos led a harvest dance.

FEATHER FROM AN INDIAN HEADDRESS

James was fast at work writing his biography, *Feather from an Indian Headdress*. By 1937 he had written 500 pages. He wrote to his former employers, telling them about the book he was writing, looking for their endorsements.

Gordon W. Lillie, "Pawnee Bill," wrote from Oklahoma:

> Friend James Deer:
>
> I surely was pleased and surprised to hear from you after so many years. I think it was back in 1884 or 1885 that I met you back in Philadelphia when I took a bunch of Indians on there to deliver to the Healy and Bigelow Sagwa Medicine Co. and it was at that time I saw you do your riding act, which I considered the greatest thing I had seen up to that time and I believe it was the greatest act I have ever seen in my life.
>
> I was awfully glad to hear from you and have this opportunity of adding my endorsement to your riding act.
>
> With best wishes I am your friend.

Another wrote:

> James Deer lifted a horse with his teeth season of 1890 with my wagon circus. Best regards to Mrs. Deer and all friends.
>
> Hastily,
> Walter L. Main
>
> Ps. When you get your script written please mail copy to Geneva, Ohio.

Esther in her notes wrote that her father had written to Prince Olaf on his visit to the United States in 1939. "Father, then ailing with a heart condition, sent him a note of welcome that he would enjoy his visit here; and on his return would he kindly give his best regards to his father, King Haakon."

In response to the letter James sent to extend a welcome on behalf of the Mohawks to Prince Olaf on his visit to the United States, he received on May 5 a letter from the prince's equerry, N. R. Ostgaard, which said the following:

H.R.H. the Crown Prince of Norway has ordered me to thank you very much for your letter of the first instant, and for the good wishes contained therein.

His Royal Highness will be glad to convey your greetings to H.M. King Haakon of Norway.

In compliance with your request I enclose a photograph of His Royal Highness the Crown Prince.

It was a kind and easy pleasure to give an old man. Prince Olaf was just a little boy interested in Indians when he asked John Deer for his picture. His father the King had taken this man as his personal guest for a tour of his countryside, and chose to sit up front next to his driver so that he could jump in and out of the car to open and close the gates of each pasture they drove through. He did this just to show James Deer, an Indian from North America, his country. Twenty nine years later that boy, now a man, could return a picture in kind. On July 10, 1939, Chief James Deer passed away.

Without her father, Esther still pursued Native American recognition. In a letter dated October 7, 1942, from the State of New York, Executive Chamber Albany, the Governor wrote:

My Dear Princess White Deer,

I'm just in receipt of your letter of your letter of September 27th. It was very thoughtful of you to write to me and I appreciate it.

I was glad to proclaim September 26th as American Indian Day. I of course cannot bind my successors to the continued observance of this day. I hope however, that they will follow my lead in this matter and continue to proclaim the day.

With best wishes, I am very sincerely yours,

Herbert H. Lehman, Governor.

PURSUIT OF THE WOLF BELT

"Figure 37 Catalog No. 37429; Size: length 32½ inches, width 4 inches; Acquired: July 24, 1898 by Mrs. Harriet M. Converse from a St. Regis Indian." So reads the 1974 Bulletin by New York State Museum of Natural History; but ever since the Akwesasne people began seeking repatriation in 1971, the Wolf Belt was removed from display and locked in a vault.

Esther continued to pursue the return and proper recognition of the Wolf Belt that the University of the State of New York and State Museum had in their possession. For up to 1971, the museum had no idea of its history of what they looked upon as a specimen in the guardianship since 1898.

Correspondence from the University of the State of New York, The State Education Department of the New York State Museum and Science Services in Albany was written to Esther on February 5, 1971, when she was nearing eighty years old.

Dear Miss Deer,

I enclose herewith the print of the wampum belt which your niece, Mrs. Trudeau, requested for you. Please be assured that my records now state that your grandfather was the hereditary bearer of this belt. Thank you for calling my attention to the note in the census book which referred to it.

Thank you for your Christmas card. It was good to hear from you again but I was sorry to read that your old family home on the reservation had been destroyed by fire. It is always sad to hear that an historic old house has been lost. It must be sadder still to have it happen to one to which one has close personal ties.

Sincerely yours
Charles E. Gillette
Curator, Archeology

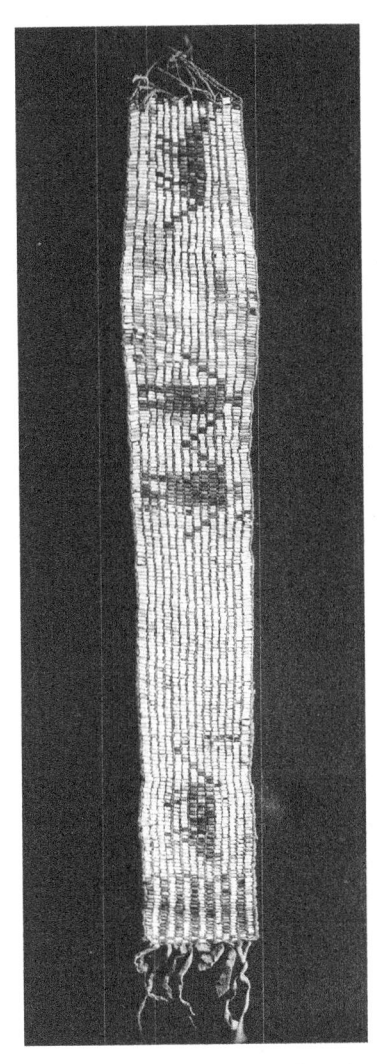

Akwesasne Wolf Belt, photographed by the State Education Department, New York State Museum and Science Service, 1971.

Her grandfather's old hotel had perished in a fire at 10:30 on the evening of December 8, 1970. The Hogansburg Fire Department responded and called Fort Covington for assistance. They responded with 12 men and equipment. The two-story International Hotel on the St. Regis reservation had been destroyed. It was one of the oldest buildings on the American-Canadian boundary; nearly 190 years old. The building had stood empty for the few months prior to the fire.

DEATH TOLLS THE DEATH OF JAMES DEER

James Deer died on July 11, 1939, at St. John's Riverside Hospital in Yonkers, New York; he was 73. A small, modest obituary appeared in the *New York Times* the next day, noting that James was a son of a Mohawk Chief who appeared in circuses and was a scout in Egypt. His death was front-page news in *The Herald Statesman* of Yonkers, and a picture of Chief Ar Ha Ken Kia Ka in his full eagle-feather headdress and deerskin tunic accompanied the story.

The last known photograph of Princess White Deer with her father, Chief James Deer, 1937.

Georgette was also a patient at the hospital at that time. She gave *The Herald Statesman* an interview from her sickbed about her husband's adventurous life. She recounted for the press how he was a descendant on his mother's side of Captain Joseph Brant, a Mohawk Chief and first cousin of Dr. Martin Orronetkaha, the founder of the Independent Order for Foresters and the builder of the Temple Building in Toronto, Canada; and how James was given the name of Ar Ha Ken Kia Ka at birth.

She validated his right to call himself chief by explaining the custom of hereditary chieftainship in which his father, Chief

Running Deer, was the last hereditary chief of the Mohawks. After him, the custom was changed to a process by which chiefs were elected for three years. On James Deer's election he was named Chief for his lifetime. He served as a Sachem of the Grand Council of the Six Nations Iroquois of the St. Regis Reservation near Roosevelttown, New York.

She retold how he was decorated by Queen Victoria and the Khedive of Egypt for his involvement in Lord Wolseley's expedition to Khartoum; how he shot the rapids of the Nile River and was a member of the first relief boat to arrive in the attempt to save the beleaguered General "Chinese" Gordon.

Georgette summarized his career, beginning with the teamwork of James and his brother, John performing as the Deer Brothers. Together they had thrilled circus-goers with their daredevil feats of trick riding, which they also performed before many of the crowned heads of Europe. Many of their stunts became standard events on rodeo programs.

She recounted his personal friendships with Jack Dempsey, the former world's heavyweight champion; Will Rogers, from his Texas Jack days; and King Haakon of Norway.

At the time of his death, James was a resident of Beech Street. His brother John was living on the St. Regis Reservation, and his daughter Leah lived with the Deer Family in Yonkers. They attended St. John's Church in Getty Square.

Had he lived, James and Georgette would have celebrated fifty years of marriage come November 18, but James had been in poor health since December and had been hospitalized three times since then. He died of heart disease.

Georgette pointed out that his constant activity on behalf of his people had undermined Chief Deer's health. She told the press that he worried when his health prevented him from journeying to Washington with a delegation from the St. Regis Reservation to consult President Roosevelt on Indian grievances. Just two years earlier he had summoned the first Grand Council of the Six Nations Iroquois since Revolutionary days.

Georgette's health had been frail most of her life. When she could not travel with her daughter, Cousin May went in her stead. Esther looked after her mother and worried over her health to the point of putting her in the hospital for a complete physical checkup for her ailments, fearing that there was something clinically wrong with her. When Esther's father died, she called upon her cousin and friend, May to come and help her. May came to her side immediately after arranging for her 14-year-old daughter, Sylvia, to be "den mother in charge" to her younger sister, brother, and her father.

THE PASSING OF THE FAMILY

In 1925, the year after Grandfather Running Deer died, his daughter Mary passed away at the age of sixty-two in St. Bartholomew's Hospital in Yonkers. Mary, Wari Sa Ta Yun Kwea or Princess Red Spear, was born in 1863 and in 1885 married Charles Williams, who was of the fifth generation of the family line of Eunice Williams, the daughter of Reverend John Williams Deerfield. Mary and Charles raised a son, Mitchell, and as owners of a business divided their time between their farmstead on the reservation, which today borders the Kahnawake Golf Course, and Birch Grove Farms in Yonkers, where they also grew and sold produce.

On June 26, 1925, shortly before Mary's death, in a rare if not singular interview, John Deer told the *Massena Observer* of his career spanning 42 years. Born on Christmas Day in 1861, the oldest of five siblings, his youngest brother and sister were now deceased; he had traveled with wagon shows as well as in modern convenience. He had been in many accidents and suffered bad injuries he was fortunate to fully recover from. The lure of the world still called to him; the call of the show and the thrill of the parade was not something easily forgotten. In 1914 he had tried to enlist in the Canadian forces, only to be turned down due to his age (he was 53). He still loved to dress in full Indian regalia and to perform dances and stage exhibitions for the delight of crowds, especially children, even after retiring.

On March 31, 1940, the year after James Deer died, his brother, John, passed away of pneumonia at the age of 79 at his home on the St. Regis Reservation. The *Yonkers Statesman* ran his obituary on April 20 in "The Final Curtain," a feature column.

The obituary recapped his father's story and continued:

> ... with his brother known as the Deer Brothers Indian Trick Riders featured with Adam Forepaugh, Barnum and Bailey, Walter L. Main, Scribner & Smith, Stowe Bros, Col. Frederick Cummings Wild West, Deer Bros. Wild West Shows with the Texas Jack Circus in South Africa. They were also featured with circuses in Germany, Russia, Poland, Denmark, Norway and Sweden... with their vaudeville sketch, 'Indians of the Past,' they played in England, Ireland, and Scotland and appeared with several dramatic companies in this country including *Daniel Boone, Checkered Life, The Great Train Robbery, The Scout, Heart of the Klondike,* and *The Flaming Arrow.* They were in several motion pictures. In 1884 the brothers were Scouts in the British Army in Egypt rescuing Lord Wolseley and were decorated by Queen Victoria. His last appearance was with the Al G. Barnes circus at the age of 75.

The only person named as his survivor was daughter, Leah Little Deer, although there was another daughter, Beatrice Jacobs of Akwesasne.

THE DEATH OF GEORGETTE DEER

Georgette Osborne Deer died at the age of 88 on her birthday on July 14, 1959. She was James' widow for 20 years. She was waked at Campbell's in New York City; a small, modest obituary ran in the *New York Times*. She was buried with her husband, her mother, and her brother.

Esther loved and honored each of her parents until their deaths. She took care of them as if they were her children.

Georgette was never left alone; the family always employed a maid and companion. Georgette was a very talented artist and excelled at sketching and painting. All her life she drew pictures of her family, and enjoyed a bit of humor in her hand-drawn Christmas cards, depicting them as three deer with Indian themes that embraced her family's heritage. Esther, too, liked to draw a deer on her Christmas cards and liked finding things with her name, like James Thurber's book, *The White Deer*.

Georgette never cut her hair. She had long beautiful hair that fell past her knees, nearly touching the floor. Esther brushed and braided it for her every day.

Georgette's only recorded performance was in Thomas Edison's *The Great Train Robbery* in 1903. She can be seen clearly in the Quadrille sequence. Her jaunty hat and recognizably unbound, lengthy hair clearly identify her.

Georgette seemed to have retired in the early 1910s after performing in Dresden. It was not noted in any newspaper that she attended any Native American events. The newspapers often noted that Chief James Deer and his daughter, Princess White Deer, were in attendance, but never mentioned Georgette. Her absence was due to her health; she still loved to hear of the adventures of her husband and daughter.

Once again Esther called on her good friend May Goodleaf to come to New York to stay with her. This time of mourning was probably hardest of all because each of the Deer Family performers had passed on, save one.

She would not have her friend May for much longer. Four short years later she would lose her too, in 1963. Marie Kaienens Splicer Goodleaf was not only her best friend but family. They were cousins through her Grandfather Running Deer's side of the family. Louis Thaeonnaienton Deer and his wife Marie Ann Aonoentsiio's daughter, Therease Kaharonkioas Deer, married J. B. Tekanakenserohen Splicer. May was their daughter.

The family ties and deep friendship still endured and were passed on to May's daughter, Sylvia Goodleaf Trudeau, who became a friend and confidante and continued hosting the annual visits to Lachine, Canada, and the telephone chats that

Princess White Deer and Sylvia Goodleaf Trudeau, 1972.

had been family tradition. Auntie Esther was a much loved and admired relative.

Esther traveled to Lachine into her 80s and was an avid golfer. She would often play with Sylvia's husband Ray, 30 years her junior, and win.

Once Esther hopped a bus to Canada and showed up at Sylvia Trudeau's door with battered luggage containing some of her treasures for safekeeping, as she unfortunately had been recently mugged in the lobby of her apartment building.

She traveled less when she reached her 90s.

LIVING TO BE ONE HUNDRED

Esther was a very giving person to anyone who came to her in need. She was known to sponsor scholarships in New York City for Mohawk students to attend college.

In 1991, in a letter to President George Bush, the chairperson of Longar Ebony Ensemble wrote that besides the fact that Esther would be awaiting a call from him on her 100th birthday, a scholarship would be sponsored for any interested Native American in the name of Princess White Deer. A small party was held in her honor near her home in Harlem.

All her life Esther said she wanted to live to be 100, and live to be 100 she did. On Thursday, October 31, *The People's Voice* ran a full-page article "Princess White Deer Turns 100 Years Old!!" highlighting her family, Wild West shows, her career as a dancer and model, the dedication of Lake Mohawk, and her life in New York City. Two pictures of her were included with the article: one at the White House in 1937, and the other with Sylvia Trudeau taken in the 1970s in Lachine, Quebec. She was still a beautiful woman.

She sang, danced, and performed before crowned heads of Europe and Russia and as far away as South Africa. She was showered with gifts, gold medallions, and pearl-handled pistols. In America she entertained members of the Rothschild family and Duke Boris of Russia. She associated with Broadway's famous.

After her 100th birthday, Esther's health began to decline. She remained at home in her apartment in a behemoth of a red stone building, The Monterey, at 114th Street and Morningside Drive, with a view south past the triangular park dedicated to Lafayette outside her second-story windows. To her west, she looked out on Morningside Park with the waterfall in view. A nurse attended to her needs as she had taken to her bed. She had lived independently and at home all of her life.

The end came quickly. She was admitted to the hospital and passed away before the family could be notified in Quebec. Esther Louise Georgette Deer had lived to be one hundred and one-quarter years old. She died on Leap Day, February 29, 1992.

Esther had wanted a big funeral, but in the end she outlived everyone she had known and loved, both on the stage and in her family, except for Sylvia.

Her funeral was very small. No obituary was published. Campbell Funeral Home on Madison Avenue handled the arrangements. A small procession left the funeral home for the cemetery in the Bronx. Only Esther's relatives, Sylvia and Ray Trudeau, and a longtime neighbor along with her daughters, attended the graveside services.

She was laid to rest in beautiful Woodlawn Cemetery on Alpine Hill beside her mother and father, Georgette and James Deer, her maternal grandmother, Mary Osborne, and her maternal uncle, Charles Osborne. A farewell letter, placed with her will, read in part:

> Death thou art but a release, the frail jar is broken that the fragrance it contains may escape and mount up to Paradise. That you my soul may live forever in the

glorious company of the Holy Spirit and with all our loved ones and the light of love, the peace and understanding and in God's loving arms the everlasting rest.

Esther went gently into that eternal sleep to join those she had known and loved in each passing era, and came to rest with those who had loved her best. While she was with us, she was aboriginally ours.

References

CHAPTER ONE: TO THE FAMILY BORN
Heritage
Blanchard, David. "For Your Entertainment Pleasure—Princess White Deer and Chief Running Deer—Last "Hereditary" Chief of the Mohawk: Northern Mohawk Rodeos and Showmanship" *Journal of Canadian Culture* 1(1984).

Bonaparte, Darren. "History of Akwesasne from Pre-Contact to Modern Times, The" and "Akwesasne Takes on the World" www.wampumchronicles.com/history.html

Birth Certificate of Esther Deer

Social Security Application of Esther Deer

United States Census. 1920. Tonawanda City, Erie County, New York.

United States Census. 1930. Rye, Westchester County, New York.

Documents Relating to the Kanien'Kehaka (Mohawk Nation)
Haudenosaunee Confederacy, The. http://sisis.nativeweb.org/6nations/main.html

Kahnawake History. http://kahnawake.com/history.asp

http://sisis.nativeweb.org/mohawk/main.html

Running Deer

Abel, Richard and Altman, Rick. "The Sounds of Early Cinema" Indiana University Press, 2001. ISBN 025333988X, 9780253339881, 327 pages.

Adams, W. Davenport. "A Dictionary of the Drama." A guide to the plays, playwrights, Players, and playhouses of the United Kingdom and America, from the earliest times to the present. Vol 1. A–G J. B. Lippincott Company, 1904. Page 203.

Baggett, James L. "A Place in Time: Wild West Comes to Birmingham" www.bplonline.org

Dodd, Thomas Allston Brown. *A History of the New York Stage from the First Performance in 1732 to 1901*. Mead and Company, New York, 1903. Page 415.

Hayesville Opera House Website. http://www.bright.net/~opera/hayesville/

Kanien'kehaka Raotitiohkwa Cultural Center, Kahnawake. From the Notes of Esther Deer. Courtesy of Sylvia Trudeau.

Klein, A. M. (Abraham Moses). Selected Poems "Indian Reservation: Caughnawaga" University of Toronto Press, 1997. Page 113.

Kronenberger, Louis. The Best Plays of 1894–1899, 1904. Page 182.

Romeo, Anthony. "Our Town" 1924. "It Seems So Long Ago"

Scrapbooks and photographs of Princess White Deer regarding George Deer. The private collection of Sylvia Trudeau. Courtesy of Sylvia Trudeau.

Age Herald, Birmingham, Alabama. February 05, 1890. "Lo, the Wild Indian"

Chateaugay Record, Quebec, Canada—New York. February 29, 1924. "Famous Indian Dies in Quebec."

Eastern Door, The, Akwesasne Mohawk Territory, New York. Volume 2, Number 5. Beauvais, Johnny. "The Golden Era Celebrities Among Us."

Gouveneur Free Press, New York. February 27, 1924. "Running Deer—Famous Indian Dies in Quebec."

News Journal, Mansfield, Ohio. August 10, 1975. Konkoly, Jim, "Old Opera House Lively."

News Journal, Mansfield, Ohio. August 20, 1976. Konkoly, Jim, "Fiddler Recalls 'Good Times.'"

New York Times, The, New York. October 20,1896. "Indians Call at City Hall."

Potsdam Herald Recorder, New York. February 29, 1924. "Running Deer Dies in Quebec."

Syracuse Herald, New York. February 23, 1924. Obituary "Mohawk's Chief Dies in Canada."

Watertown Daily Times, New York. February 22, 1924. Obituary

Watertown Daily Times, New York. February 26, 1924. Obituary

Watertown Daily News, New York. February 22, 1924. "Famous Indian Dies in Quebec."

Robinson's

Old Fulton Post Card. www.fultonhistory.com

Buffalo Express, The, New York. Tuesday Morning, February 17, 1891.

Illustrated Buffalo Express, The, New York. Morning Edition, February 15, 1891.

New York Clipper, The, New York. February 23, 1888.

New York Clipper, The, New York. February 23, 1891.

Umatillia Tonic

Medicine Man Show http://mcadamsmagic.com/medicineman.htm

Old Fulton Post Card. www.fultonhistory.com
Dallas Morning News, July 15, 1901.
Decature Daily Republican, The. 1892.
Kingston Daily Freeman. New York. July 15, 16, 1901.
Malone Palladium, The. New York. 1891.
New York Clipper, The. New York. July 29, 1883.
New York Clipper, The. New York. August 11, 1887–1888.
New York Clipper, The. New York. February 23, 1888.
New York Clipper, The. New York. 1888–1889
New York Clipper, The. New York. April 20, 1888–1890.
New York Clipper, The. New York. May 4, 1888–1890.
New York Clipper, The. New York. June 27, 1890–1891.
New York Clipper, The. New York. July 9, 1891.
New York Clipper, The. New York. October 10, 1891–1893.
New York Clipper, The. New York. November 21, 1891.
New York Clipper, The. New York. July 12, 1914–1915.
Ogdensburg Advance, The. New York. August 17, 1893.
St. Lawrence Herald. Potsdam, New York. Friday, August 6, 1897.

Pan-American Exposition
Notes on the Pan-American Exposition by Robert Grant.
The Cosmopolitan, September 1901. http://www.nps.gov/archive/thri/home.htm
"Doing the Pan." Pan-American Exposition. 1901 Buffalo. http://panam1901.bfn.org/sitemap.htm.
Pan-American Exposition Links: Theodore Roosevelt Inaugural National Historic Site http://www.nps.gov/archive/thri/home.htm
Arnold, C. E. Official photographer for the Pan-American Exposition. National Archives, Washington, D.C., and Akwesasne Cultural Center, Akwesasne Mohawk Territory, New York. *Buffalo Express, The.* New York. June 9, 1901.

The Quiet Life
Old Fulton Post Card. www.fultonhistory.com
Ogdensburg Advance, The. New York. July 30, 1897.
Malone Palladium, The. New York. Thursday, August 5, 1897.

Akwesasne Wolf Belt
Bonaparte, Chief Darren. "What You Don't Know, and Why You Don't Know It: The Hidden History of the Seven Nations of Canada." *The Wampum Chronicles*, www.wampumchronicles.com

Fenton, William S. "The New York State Wampum Collection: The Case for the Integrity of Cultural Treasures" Proceedings of the American Philosophical Society, The American Philosophical Society. Independence Square, Philadelphia 1971. Pages 437 – 461.

Kanien'kehaka Raotitiohkwa Cultural Center, Kahnawake. From the Notes of Esther Deer. Courtesy of Sylvia Trudeau.

University of the State of New York, The State Education Department, New York State Museum and Science Services Correspondence to Esther Deer and Sylvia Trudeau, February 5, 1971.

Indian Time, Akwesasne Mohawk Territory, New York. Volume 14, Number 23. June 14, 1996. Page 20.

Indian Time, Akwesasne Mohawk Territory, New York.

Wampum Belts. Pamphlet produced by Six Nations Indian Museum Onchiota, New York.

James Deer
The Herald Statesman. Yonkers, New York. July 11, 1939. Obituary "Chief of Mohawks Dies Here At 73."

Khartoum

Deer, James D. "The Canadian Voyageurs in Egypt" Published by J. Lovell, 1885. ISBN 0665540159, 9780665540158. Reproduction of original in: New Brunswick Museum.

Jackson, Louis. "Our Caughnawagas in Egypt." Published by William Drysdale & Co. 1885. Original from Harvard University. Digitized Jun 17, 2008.

McIntyre, James. "Poems by James McIntyre," 1889. "Canadian Voyageurs on the Nile." Page 29.

Moses, John with Graves, Donald and Sinclair, Warren. "A Sketch Account of Aboriginal Peoples in The Canadian Military" ©Minister of National Defense Canada, 2004. Available only in electronic form, Pages 50–56.

Thomas, Don, Warrant Officer (retired). "Canadian Military Engineers Throughout History" and "Canadians In The Sudan" http://collections.ic.gc.ca./heirloom_series/volume5/82-85.htm

BBC—History—Historic Figures—General Charles Gordon www.bbc.co.uk/history

Nile River Expedition 1884–1885. Canadian Boatmen Challenge the Nile www.artiquesroadshow.com/Medals

Veterans Affairs Canada, Anciens Combattants Canada, VAC Canada Remembers, Egypt Medal (1884–1885) www.vac-acc.gc.ca

Kanien'kehaka Raotitiohkwa Cultural Center, Kahnawake.
From the Notes of James Deer. Courtesy of Sylvia Trudeau.

Georgette Deer

Kanien'kehaka Raotitiohkwa Cultural Center, Kahnawake.
From the Notes of Esther Deer. Courtesy of Sylvia Trudeau.

Uncle Tom's Cabin (UTC) http://etext.lib.virginia.edu/railton/

Slout, William L. Compiled and Edited "Olympians of the Sawdust Circle: A biographical dictionary of the nineteenth century American circus" Copyright © 2005. All rights reserved.

CHAPTER TWO: WILD WEST SHOWS
Daniel Boone—Indians of the Past

Deer, Esther White, (Os-Ka-Non-Do). "An Explanation of the Wampum Belt" a paper within the Notes of Esther Deer. Kanien'kehaka Raotitiohkwa Cultural Center, Kahnawake. Courtesy of Sylvia Trudeau.

Kanien'kehaka Raotitiohkwa Cultural Center, Kahnawake. From the Notes of Esther Deer regarding Captain Jack Crawford. Courtesy of Sylvia Trudeau.

Herald Statesman, The. Yonkers, New York. July 11, 1939. "Chief of Mohawks Dies Here At 73."

Old Fulton Post Card. www.fultonhistory.com

Auburn Bulletin, The. Auburn, New York. Saturday, December 15, 1888. "Quarrelsome Indians."

Brooklyn Daily Eagle, The. New York. Sunday, April 16, 1933. "George M. Cohan the Man Who Refuses to Be Standardized."

Brooklyn Daily Eagle, The. New York. Saturday, December 15, 1888. "Wild Warfare."

Brooklyn Daily Eagle, The. New York. Sunday, December 16, 1888.

Rochester Democratic Chronicle, New York. Sunday Morning, December 16, 1888. "They Had a Real Fight."

Evening Telegram, The. New York. Saturday, December 15, 1888. "The Realistic Drama."

Evening Telegram, The. New York. January 22, 1889.

Gazette and Farmer Journal, The. New York. January 31, 1889.
Poughkeepsie Daily Eagle. New York. January 23, 1889
Roman Citizen. New York. April 10, 1889.
St. Lawrence Plain Dealer, The. Canton, New York
Brooklyn Daily Eagle, The. New York. Sunday, April 24, 1889.
Powers, Mabel. "Stories the Iroquois Tell Their Children" "How Two Indian Boys Settled a Quarrell" New York. American Book Company. 1917.
Queen's Theatre Programme. 714 East High Street, Poplar. England. Week of Easter Monday, April 16, 1906. Deer Family. "Indians of the Past" 4th billing.

The Great Train Robbery

Edison, Thomas. Edison Manufacturing Co., 1903. *The great train robbery* / Thomas A. Edison, Inc. ; producer, Edwin S. Porter. http://tw.video.yahoo.com/video/play?vid=590005
Old Fulton Post Card. www.fultonhistory.com
New York Clipper, The. New York. February 6, 1903–1904. Great Train Robbery Advertisement.
New York Clipper, The. New York. July 25, 1903–1904. Great Train Robbery Advertisement.

Queen of the Highway

Old Fulton Post Card. www.fultonhistory.com
New York Clipper, The. New York. March 28, 1896–1897.
New York Clipper, The. New York. January 31, 1903.
New York Clipper, The. New York. July 25, 1903–1904. Toronto Fair Advertisement.
Poughkeepsie Daily Eagle. New York. Monday, January 5, 1903.
Poughkeepsie Daily Eagle. New York. Tuesday, January 6, 1903.

Rochester Democrat and Chronicle. New York. Sunday, January 25, 1903.
Rochester Democrat and Chronicle. New York. Thursday, January 29, 1903.
Rochester Democrat and Chronicle. New York. Friday, January 30, 1903.
Syracuse Post Standard. New York. Tuesday Morning, February 9, 1904.
Utica Herald-Dispatch. New York. Saturday Evening, January 14, 1903.
Utica Herald-Dispatch. New York. Friday Evening, February 20, 1903.
Utica Herald-Dispatch. New York. Saturday Evening, February 21, 1903.
Utica Herald-Dispatch. New York. Monday Evening, February 23, 1903.
Utica Herald-Dispatch. New York. Tuesday Evening, February 24, 1903.
Utica Sunday Tribune, The. New York. February 22, 1903.
Pittsburg Press, The, Pennsylvania. May 24, 1903. The Coming Shows. Bijou.

Texas Jack's Wild West Show—South Africa

Buffalo Bill History "Buffalo Bill's Life" www.buffalbill.org/history.htm

Kanien'kehaka Raotitiohkwa Cultural Center, Kahnawake. From the Notes of Esther Deer regarding South Africa and Texas Jack. Courtesy of Sylvia Trudeau.

Handbook of Texas Online: Omohundro, John Burwell, JR. www.tsha.utexas.edu/handbook/online/articles

Schulte. Melvin. "Buffalo Bill as Reported in the Newspapers" www.historybuff.com/library/refbuffalo.html

Wild West Shows—The 101 Ranch www.jcs-group.com/oldwewt/show/rogerswill.html

Will Rogers Bio—Will Rogers Motion Picture Pioneer Foundation. http://www.wrpioneers.org

Copyrighted Act

Library of Congress Patent No 7394, Kanien'kehaka Raotitiohkwa Cultural Center Collection, courtesy of Sylvia Trudeau.

Kanien'kehaka Raotitiohkwa Cultural Center, Kahnawake. From an Undated Scrapbook of the Deer Family. Courtesy of Sylvia Trudeau.

Scrapbooks and photographs of Princess White Deer, Original Copyright Document. The private collection of Sylvia Trudeau. Courtesy of Sylvia Trudeau.

Walter Main

Circus Historical Society, Who's Who in the American Circus. Sturtevant's List of Circuses, 1880–1889 Walter Main's.

East London Theatre Archive project, University of East London. Queen's Theatre, Poplar (London, England) 1906 Theater Programme for Week beginning Easter Monday, 16 April 1906. "Deer Family, Genuine North American Indians in their sensational act, "Indians of the Past""

Kanien'kehaka Raotitiohkwa Cultural Center, Kahnawake. From the Notes of Esther Deer 1901 through 1909. Courtesy of Sylvia Trudeau.

Letter from the Scrapbook of the Esther Deer. The private collection of Sylvia Trudeau. Courtesy of Sylvia Trudeau.

Old Fulton Post Card. www.fultonhistory.com

Daily Mirror, The. New York. September 2, 1908. "Comedian's Fabulous Salary," picture of Lauder, James Deer, John Deer, and Princess White Deer

New York Clipper, The. May 26, 1893. "Under the White Tents"—Walter Main. Thrown during train accident

New York Clipper, The. New York. June 9, 1893. Walter Main.

New York Clipper, The. New York. May 26, 1896.

New York Clipper, The. New York. March 28, 1896. "Under the White Tents"—Walter Main.

New York Clipper, The. New York. August 11, 1887–1888.

Dresden Germany

Dictionary of Canadian Biography, Pages 137–139.

Some Descendants of Joseph Brant by J. Ojijatekha Brant-Sero, Ontario Historic Society, Papers and Records, Vol. 1, Published in Toronto in 1899, Pages 113–117.

Kreis, Karl Markus. "Prinzessin Esther White Deer in Dresden," 1910.

Karl May Wiki. www.wikipedia.org and www://en.wikipedia.org/wiki/KarlMay

Kanien'kehaka Raotitiohkwa Cultural Center, Kahnawake. From the 1910 news clipping from the scrapbook of Esther Deer. Courtesy of Sylvia Trudeau.

Kanien'kehaka Raotitiohkwa Cultural Center, Kahnawake. Zoological Gardens Dresden, January 10 and 13 undated clipping from scrapbook of Esther Deer. Courtesy of Sylvia Trudeau.

The End of the Act—Indians of the Past

Boston Globe, Massachussets. "Juggling Between Acts How a Big Apple Family Handles Life in a Three Generation Circus," Negri, Gloria, Globe Staff. April 27, 1993.

New York Times. New York. December 28, 2004. Obituary of Max Schumann.

New York Times. New York. February 12, 2005. Lives in Brief—Max Schumann

Britannica Online Encyclopedia, Circus: History. www.Britannica.com

CircusNews.com / News.SimplyCircus.com

Cooper, Diane Starr. "Night After Night" www.cirkusskandinavia.dk/schumannprg2.htm

New York Times. New York. December 28, 2004. Obituary of Max Schumann.

New York Times. New York. February 12, 2005. Lives in Brief—Max Schumann.

Scrapbooks and photographs of Princess White Deer. The private collection of Sylvia Trudeau. Courtesy of Sylvia Trudeau.

Wikipedia, the free encyclopedia. Albert Schumann Theatre. www.wikipedia.com

CHAPTER THREE: A CAREER OF HER OWN
From Russia With Love

The Papoose, Lake Mohawk, New Jersey. "Princess White Deer Today" by Audrey Smolik, May, 1981. Pages 23, 24.

Kanien'kehaka Raotitiohkwa Cultural Center, Kahnawake. Diplomatic Documents as Wards of the United States. Scrapbooks of Princess White Deer. Courtesy of Sylvia Trudeau.

Wikipedia.org—Haakon VII of Norway. www.wikipedia.com

A Brief Marriage

Society of the American Indians, "The American Indian Magazine" published as The Quarterly Journal of the Society of American Indians. Vol. IV. January–March 1916 Pages 197, 198.

Genealogia Dynastyczna (Dynastic Genealogy). Dynasties and Aristocratic Families. Aristocratic family Krasicki coat of arms Rogala. http://genealog.pl

Daily Herald, The. Chicago, Illinois. November, 1915.

Fitchburg Daily Sentinel, The. Massachusetts. June 22, 1915.

Lincoln Sunday Star, The, "Indian Princess to Wed an Officer in Russian Army."

Malone Farmer, The. New York. December 29, 1915.

Old Fulton Post Card. www.fultonhistory.com

Post Standard, The. Syracuse, New York. Wednesday Morning, September 22, 1915. "Mohawk Indian Princess is Bride of Count Krasicka, Russian Nobleman."

Syracuse Journal. New York. June 21, 1915. "Princess To Marry Russian Count."

Illustrated Buffalo Express, The. New York. September 12, 1915.

Democratic Chronicle, Rochester, New York. Sunday, June 20, 1915. "Mohawk Indian Princess to Wed Russian Count."

Scrapbooks and photographs of Princess White Deer, The private collection of Sylvia Trudeau. Photographic Postcard correspondence from Count Alex Krasicki. March 30, 1912; October 27, 1912; and July 28, 1913. Postcard correspondence from Esther Deer to her parents from Kiev, March 18, 1916. Postcard correspondence from Esther Deer, Tonawanda, New York to May Splicer, Montreal, Canada. Postmarked July 17, 1916. Courtesy of Sylvia Trudeau.

Keith—Vaudeville

Jessup, Lynda. ed. Toronto. "Antimodernism and Artistic Experience: Policing the Boundaries of Modernity" University of Toronto Press, 2001. Page 37.

Kenrick, John. *A History of The Musical Vaudeville,* Copyright 1996–2004. Musicals101.com

Samuels, C. and Samuels, L. *Once Upon a Stage* (New York: Dodd, Mead & Co, 1974), p. 89.

Stein, Charles W. ed., *American Vaudeville as Seen by its Contemporaries,* New York, Alfred Knopf. 1984.

Tucker, Sophie. *Some of These Days.* Pages 148–149.

Theatre Magazine. January, 1921. "All the World Dancing Mad."
Theatre Magazine. April 1923. "The Two-A-Day."
Internet Broadway Database: Hippodrome Theatre Details. www.IBDB.com
The Keith/Albee Collection: The Vaudeville Industry. 1894–1935, The University of Iowa Libraries, Special Collections. By M. Alison Kibler from Books at Iowa 56 (April 1992) University of Iowa. www.lib.uioa.edu/
Kanien'kehaka Raotitiohkwa Cultural Center, Kahnawake. Newsclippings. undated from the scrapbook of Esther Deer. "Original Americans Head the Vaudeville Bill at the Grand;" "Amusements Keith Vaudeville at the Lyric," Atlanta, GA.; and Variety Magazine. Undated. Keith's Atlantic City Advertisement. Courtesy of Sylvia Trudeau.
Lazer Vaudeville's Curriculum-Based Study Guide & Lesson Plan. http://www.lazervaudeville.com/
Old Fulton Post Card. www.fultonhistory.com
  Brooklyn Daily Eagle, The. New York. October 16, 1917. The Flatbush Theatre.
  Brooklyn Daily Eagle, The. New York. January 11, 1925. The Hippodrome Houdini.
New York Clipper, The. New York. August 3, 1917.
New York Clipper, The. New York. August 3, 1917.
New York Clipper, The. New York. September 12, 1917.
New York Clipper, The. New York. September 19, 1917.
New York Clipper, The. New York. October 16, 1917.
New York Clipper, The. New York. October 21, 1917.
New York Clipper, The. New York. October 24, 1917.
New York Clipper, The. New York. October 31, 1917.
New York Clipper, The. New York. November 2, 1917.
New York Clipper, The. New York. November 7, 1917.
New York Clipper, The. New York. November 14, 1917.
New York Clipper, The. New York. November 21, 1917.

New York Clipper, The. New York. November 28, 1917.
New York Clipper, The. New York. December 5, 1917.
New York Clipper, The. New York. December 12, 1917.
New York Clipper, The. New York. December 19, 1917.
New York Clipper, The. New York. December 26, 1917.
New York Clipper, The. New York. January 2, 1918.
New York Clipper, The. New York. January 9, 1918.
New York Clipper, The. New York. June 5, 1918.
New York Clipper, The. New York. July 24, 1918.
New York Clipper, The. New York. December 4, 1918.
New York Clipper, The. New York. March 19, 1919. Proctor's Yonkers. Pages 21 and 27.
Evening Telegram, The. New York. Sept.–Oct. 1920. "Won Her Way to the very "Tip Top"
New York Times, The. "Gossip of the Vaudeville Stage" November 9, 1924.
New York Times, The. January 11, 1925. Photo Standalone Page RP6.
Syracuse Journal. New York. Friday, August 3, 1917.
Syracuse Journal. New York. Friday, August 4, 1917.
Syracuse Post Standard. New York. August 4, 1917.
Trenton Evening Times. New Jersey. State Street Theatre. February 11, 1919.

A Family Evening Turned Bad
Old Fulton Post Card. www.fultonhistory.com
Buffalo Express, The. New York. March 28, 1917 "Girl Released in Lawyer's Custody. Man whom she shot says she was justified—He is in fair way to recover"
Buffalo Express, The. New York. March 31, 1917.
Buffalo Express, The. New York. April 4, 1917.
Lowville Journal Republican, Buffalo area, New York. 1917.
Monroe County Mail, The. New York. October 25, 1917.

Peppy De Albrew—Atlantic City Dance

Battay, Ethel. "Hotel Echoes." Page 15, description of Peppy's clothing.

Kanien'kehaka Raotitiohkwa Cultural Center, Kahnawake. From the Scrapbooks of Esther Deer. unknown newspaper, of unknown date. "Supper Dances Have Opening At Ambassador." Courtesy of Sylvia Trudeau.

Valentino: Recollections of Sylvia Trudeau as told to her by Princess White Deer.

Wikipedia, the free encyclopedia, definition of Pépé le Moko. www.wikipedia.com

Coshocton Tribune, The. Ohio. November 9, 1957. Dorothy Kilgallen Column. Page 4.

Charleston Daily Mail. West Virginia. March 17, 1935.

Charleston Gazette, The. Charleston, West Virginia. Sunday, July 6, 1924.

Galveston Daily News, The. Galveston, Texas. October 20, 1957.

Gettysburg Times, The. August 29, 1935.

Hammond Times, The. Indiana. February 13, 1934. "My New York" Column by James Aswell. Page 4.

Humboldt Standard. August 6, 1957. "New York Confidential" by Lee Mortimer. Page 4.

Old Fulton Post Card. www.fultonhistory.com

Lethbridge Herald, The. December 30, 1932. Page 2.

Lowell Sun, The. Lowell, Massachusetts. October 12, 1944. Dorothy Kilgallen Column. Page 21.

Lowell Sun, The. Lowell, Massachusetts. September 23, 1952. Dorothy Kilgallen Column.

Lowell Sun, The. Lowell, Massachusetts. January 16, 1956. Dorothy Kilgallen Column. Page 14.

Lowell Sun, The. Lowell, Massachusetts. June 4, 1969.

Mansfield News-Journal. Ohio. April 15, 1941. Broadway by Dorothy Kilgallen. Page 9.

Modesto Bee and News – Herald, The. California. February 26, 1937.
News, The. Frederick, Maryland. October 19, 1934.
New York Times. New York. June 18, 1924.
New York Times. New York. June 19, 1924.
Port Arthur News, The. Port Arthur, Texas. May 20, 1931. "On Broadway" by Winchell, Walter. Page 4.
Port Arthur News, The. Port Arthur, Texas. November 1, 1934. "Broadway" by Winchell, Walter.
Times, The. San Mateo, California. May 20, 1959.

From Wigwam to White Lights

Kanien'kehaka Raotitiohkwa Cultural Center, Kahnawake. Scrapbooks and photographs of Esther Deer. Courtesy of Sylvia Trudeau.
New York Variety. New York. January 21, 1925.
New York American. New York. March 15, 1925.
The Sphere. April 18, 1925.
Unknown newspaper. Undated. "Keith Star Ordered South."
Brooklyn Daily Eagle. New York. January 11, 1925.
Miami Daily News and Metropolis. Florida. Wednesday, March 31, 1926. "Charleston makes small hit with this Seminole Matron."
Morning Telegraph, The. Saturday, March 7, 1925. "Princess White Deer Suffers Breakdown Preparing Act."

Dancing on the Radio

Camurat, Diane, "The American Indian in The Great War." Chapter Two: American Indian Service In WWI, 2.2.1. Recruiting Agents.
Le Miroir. France. June 17, 1917. Chief Eagle Horse photo on Wall Street. *Le Miroir.* June 17, 1917.

Kanien'kehaka Raotitiohkwa Cultural Center, Kahnawake.

Scrapbooks and photographs of Esther Deer. Courtesy of Sylvia Trudeau and Scrapbooks and photographs of Princess White Deer, The private collection of Sylvia Trudeau. Courtesy of Sylvia Trudeau.

Western Union Telegram, March 25, 1925, from Mark Luescher to Princess White Deer.

Programme of the Testimonial Performance in Honor of General John J. Pershing, Saturday Evening, April 25, 1925.

Massachusetts newspaper clipping. April 25, 1925.

Ziegfeld

1920's Stage Chronology, Musicals101.com http://www.musicals101.com/1920s.htm Ziegfeld 9 O'clock Frolic (3rd ed.)

American Musical Theatre: A Chronicle Second Edition, by Gerald Bordman. New York, Oxford: Oxford University Press, 1992. Page 350.

Barat, Robert. "Revue: a Nostalgic reprise of the great Broadway period" New York: Fleet Pub. Corp. 1st ed. Pages 53–57.

Burns Mantle, The Best Plays of 1921–1922, "Ziegfeld Follies of 1921."

Burton, Jack. "The Blue Book of Broadway Musicals," Watkins Glen, New York. Century House, 1969.

Cinephillacs Movie Forum, www.cinephiacs.com

"Here We Are" Broadway Musicals http://erga.packhum.org/broadway/shows

IBDB Internet Broadway Database www.ibdb.com New Amsterdam Roof, Ziegfeld 9 O'clock Frolic.

Official Metropolitan Guide published for the Hotel Association of New York City. Week of February 20, 1921. Page 33, photo advertisement Page 28.

Magazine Theatre Program for Ziegfeld Roof, Ziegfeld Midnight Frolic; copyright New York Theatre Program Corporation 1921. Pages 13, 17, 19, 22, and 23.

Modern Theatre Online: Productions, http://www.moderntheatre.info

Old Fulton Post Card. www.fultonhistory.com

Binghampton Press, The. New York. Tuesday Evening, March 19, 1921.

New York Clipper, The. New York. January 26, 1921.

New York Evening Telegram. New York. February, 6, 1921.

New York Evening Telegram. New York. March 6, 1921.

New York Evening Telegram. New York. April 3, 1921.

New York Evening Telegram. New York. January 22, 1921

New York Evening Telegram. New York. February 20, 1921.

New York Evening Telegram. New York. March 27, 1921.

New York Tribune. New York. February 6, 1921.

New York Times, The. New York. February 6, 1921.

Scrapbooks and photographs of Princess White Deer, Erlanger Dillingham Ziegfeld Concert From the scrapbook of Esther Deer, playbill from New Amsterdam Theatre, Sunday, Nov. 9, 1919, Third of the Series. The private collection of Sylvia Trudeau. Courtesy of Sylvia Trudeau.

Second Seattle Review Program. Thursday, November 7, 1918.

Ziegfeld 101: The Follies http://www.musicals101.com/ziegfollies3.htm Kerick, John. "Ziegfield 101" 2003.

The Ziegfeld Club, Inc. www.thenationalziegfeldclubinc.com

Not without my Permission—
The Astute Business Woman

New York Times, The. New York,. March 5, 1921. "Princess White Deer gets Court Order."

Old Fulton Post Card. www.fultonhistory.com

Brooklyn Daily Eagle. New York. March 6, 1921. "A Cruel Indian Princess."

Morning Express. Buffalo, New York. March 5, 1921. "Would Stop Magazine—Woman charges picture on book cover is her portrait."

Morning Express. Buffalo, New York. March 7, 1921.

Broadway
Hitchy-Koo 1919

Albert Von Tilzer, His Life & Music. Https://parlorsongs.com

Bordman, Gerald Martin."American Musical Theatre, A Chronicle." New York. Oxford University Press, 1992. Page 342.

Burns Mantle, The Best Plays of 1919 – 1920. Page 366.

Camurat, Diane. "The American Indian in the Great War, Real and Imagined." 1996. www.lib.byu.edu/estu/wwi/comment.cmrts

Chicago Daily Tribune. Illinois. February 18, 1920. Percy Hammond "Hitch" Photo.

Detroit Journal. Michigan. December 24, 1919.

Ewen, David. "American songwriters: An H.W. Wilson biographical dictionary." Page 294.

Fulton Patriot. New York. January 2, 1920.

"Here We Are" Broadway Musicals www.erga.packhum.org/broadway/shows Hitchy-Koo 1919.

IBDB Internet Broadway Database www.ibdb.com

Mementos and scrapbooks of May Splicer Greenleaf. "Moonlight." The private collection of Sylvia Trudeau. Courtesy of Sylvia Trudeau.

Mid-week Pictorial. New York. October 21, 1920.

Modesto Evening News, The. California. May 1, 1920.

New York Times, The. New York. July 30, 1921.

New York Times, The. New York. November 19, 1919.

Ogden Standard Examiner, The. Utah. April 12, 1920.

Old Fulton Post Card. www.fultonhistory.com

 Illustrated Buffalo Morning Express, The. November 10, 1919. "Indian Princess is everything."

 New York Clipper, The. New York. July 30, 1919. "Hitchy-Koo Aug. 18."

 New York Clipper, The. New York. November 5, 1919.

 Evening Telegram, The. New York. Sept.–Oct. 1920. "Won Her Way to the very "Tip Top."

 New York Evening Telegram. New York October 5, 1919.

 New York Evening Telegram. New York October 7, 1919.

 Brooklyn Daily Eagle. New York. August 10, 1919.

 Brooklyn Daily Eagle. New York. October 7, 1919.

 Rochester Democrat and Chronicle. New York. January 4, 1920.

 Fulton Patriot. January 7, 1920.

 Buffalo Morning Express. New York. November 20, 1919

Playbill News: Today in Theatre History October 6. www.playbills.com/news/article "Best Plays of 1919 to 1920 and the Year Book of Drama in America." Burns.

Sunday Star. December 21, 1919.

Washington Post, The. District of Columbia. October 5, 1919.

Washington State University, Wallis & Marilyn Kimble Northwest History Database 1013-04-11 (Chief Eagle Horse) www.wsulibs.wsu.edu

Toledo Blade. Ohio. November 22, 1919.

Tip Top

Bordman, Gerald. "American Musical Theatre A Chronicle." New York. Oxford University Press, 1992. Pages 354–355.

Internet Broadway Database www.ibdb.com

Mid-week Pictorial Magazine, The. New York. October 21, 1920.

Munsey's Magazine. Published 1921. Original from the University of Michigan. Digitized December 5, 2008. Page 700.

Old Fulton Post Card. www.fultonhistory.com

Evening Telegram, The. New York. Sept.–Oct. 1920. "Won Her Way to the very "Tip Top."

New York Clipper, The. New York. September 22, 1920. "Fred Stone Show Opens."

New York Clipper, The. New York. October 13, 1920.

Time Mid-week Pictorial. New York. July 7, 1936.

Time Magazine. New York. http://www.time.com/time/magazine/article/0,9171,847827,00.html

Vermazen, Bruce. "That moaning saxophone: the Six Brown Brothers and the dawning of a musical." 2004. Pages 145, 146.

The Yankee Princess

"bajadere" Wikipedia, the free encyclopedia—definition. www.wikipedia.org

IBDB Internet Broadway Database www.ibdb.com

Martin, Jessie Wright. "A Survey of the Operettas of Emmerich Kálmán." 2005.

Old Fulton Post Card. www.fultonhistory.com

New York Evening Telegram. New York. October 3, 1922. "Yankee Princess a Real Musical Treat"

Hilton Record. Hilton, New York. Jan.–Oct. 1922.

New York Daily Telegram. New York. Sept.–Oct. 1920.

New York Evening Telegram. New York. October 1, 1922.

New York Evening Telegram. New York. October 13, 1922.

New York Evening Telegram. New York. October 22, 1922.

New York Tribune. New York. October 1, 1922.

Lucky

Bordman, Gerald. "American Musical Theatre: A Chronicle." New York. Oxford University Press, 1992. Page 423.

Burns Mantle, "The Best Plays of 1926–27." Pages 14, 495.
Daily News, The. Frederick, Maryland. April 8, 1927.
Decatur Review, The. Decatur, Ilinois. Sunday, March 27, 1927.
IBDB Internet Broadway Database www.ibdb.com
"Here We Are" Broadway Musicals http://erga.packhum.org/broadway/shows Lucky
Lima Sunday News, The. Ohio. March 27, 1927.
Lowell Sun, The. Lowell Massachusetts. March 28, 1927.
New York Times, The. New York. May 1, 1927.
Old Fulton Post Card. www.fultonhistory.com
  Brooklyn Daily Eagle. New York. March 23, 1927. "Plays and Things" by Arthur Pollock. "Mary Eaton and Paul Whitean in 'Lucky' Latest of Charles Dillingham's Elaborate Musical Comedies."
Syracuse Herald, The. New York. May 1, 1927.

Paris 1928

Bismarck Tribune, The. North Dakota. "Pictures Flashes Out Of The Day's News From Around The World." March 30, 1929.
Kanien'kehaka Raotitiohkwa Cultural Center, Kahnawake. From the Notes of Esther Deer. Undated, 1928, clipping "Real Indian Princess Paris Favorite." Courtesy of Sylvia Trudeau.
Old Fulton Post Card. www.fultonhistory.com
  Brooklyn Daily Eagle. New York. Thursday, March 21, 1929. "Indian Actress Home."
Scrapbooks and photographs of Princess White Deer, The private collection of Sylvia Trudeau. Courtesy of Sylvia Trudeau.
  Correspondence: Ziegfeld Office. August 13, 1928. Walter Kingsley to Mr. Beth Beri.
  Correspondence: Il de France Chief Purser onboard to Princess White Deer regarding rehearsals with Delores Rio.

Il de France Manifest of First Class Passengers.

CHAPTER FOUR: THE LAKE MOHAWK CONNECTION

Courier Freeman. Potsdam, St. Lawrence County, New York. June 27, 1927. Section 2.

Dunn, Judy. "Lake Mohawk Reflections" 2002. Lake Mohawk Country Club. USA.

Lake Mohawk Papoose, The. Sparta, New Jersey. July 30, 1932.

Lake Mohawk Papoose, The. Sparta, New Jersey. Sept 24, 1932.

Lake Mohawk Papoose, The. Sparta, New Jersey. June, 1937.

Lake Mohawk Papoose, The. Sparta, New Jersey. August/September, 1937.

Pierson, Ph.D., Duane. "Images of Sparta." 1981. Minisink Press Inc. Newton, New Jersey. Pages 50–51.

Old Fulton Post Card. www.fultonhistory.com

Brooklyn Daily Eagle, The. New York. Friday, May 6, 1927. "Today's Radio Program" Lacrosse.

Brooklyn Daily Eagle, The. New York. Sunday, May 8, 1927. "Today's Radio Program." American Indian Songs.

Brooklyn Daily Eagle. The. New York Sunday, May 29, 1927. "Today's Radio Program." An American Indian Idyll.

Brooklyn Daily Eagle. The. New York. July 28, 1927 "Today's Radio Program."

Brooklyn Daily Eagle, The. New York. Sunday. August 14, 1932/ "Lake Mohawk Club Has Busy Schedule."

Niagara Falls Gazette. New York. Thursday, May 26, 1927. "Navy Yard Band from WNYC."

Pierson, Ph.D., Duane. "Images of Sparta" 1981. Minisink Press Inc. Newton, New Jersey. Pages 50–51.

Pittsburgh Post-Gazette. Pennsylvania. August 24, 1932.

Postsdam Courier. New York. June 29, 1927. "Indian Princess Visits Former Hogansburg Home."

Scrapbooks and photographs of Princess White Deer. Closs, Herbert L. Letter to Princess White Deer, Lachine, Quebec July 3, 1979. The private collection of Sylvia Trudeau. Courtesy of Sylvia Trudeau.

CHAPTER FIVE: ARTISTS AND SCHOLARS
Arnold Genthe
The AMICO Library www.davidrumsey.com (photos 3)
New York Historical Society http://dlib.nyu.edu Guide to the Arnold Genthe Photograph Collection (1895–1942)
www.Wikipedia.org/wiki/Arnold_Genthe

E. O. Hoppé
Bee, The. Danville, Virginia. November 7, 1922.
Fort Wayne Journal-Gazette, The. Fort Wayne, Indiana. December 16, 1922.
La Cross Tribune and Leader Press. La Cross, Wisconsin. November 14, 1922.
Modesto Evening News, The. Modesto, California. November 10, 1922.
Ogden Standard Examiner, The. Ogden, Utah. November 5, 1922.
Scrapbooks and photographs of Princess White Deer, The private collection of Sylvia Trudeau. Courtesy of Sylvia Trudeau.
  Correspondence: Cooper Union for the Advancement of Science and Art. January 28,1920 to Princess White Deer.
  Correspondence: Famous Players—Lasky Corporation, Paramount Pictures, 485 Fifth Avenue, New York City, New York. May 27, 1925 to Princess White Deer.
Utica Observer, New York.1922.

Music
Syncopation
Hoppé, Michael and Wheater,Tim."The Yearning: Romances for Alto Flute" "Indigo Sunset (For Princess White Deer)." October 22, 1996. 5:40 Audio CD.

New Grove Dictionary of Jazz, The. Paul Whiteman. Oxford University Press. http://www.pbs.org/jazz/biography/artist_id_whiteman_paul.htm

Utica Herald Dispatch. New York. April 16, 1920. Heale, James. "Indian Tomtoms started Jazz On its Syncopated Fury."

Warren Tribune, The. Warren, Pennsylvania. May 11, 1927. Abbott, Amy "Her Day of Work and Play."

Scholars
Billboard Year Book of the New York Legitimate Stage, The. Original from Stanford University. Page 33.

Baral, Robert. "Revue: A Nostalgic Reprise of the Great Broadway Period." Page 55.

Blanchard, David Scott. "For your entertainment and pleasure—Princess White Deer and Chief Running Deer—last "hereditary" chief of the Mohawk: Northern Mohawk rodeos and showmanship" 1984. Bowling Green University Popular Press. 18 pages. *Journal of Canadian Culture* *1*(1984): 99–116.

Bordman, Gerald Martin. "American Musical Theatre: A Chronicle." Page 342.

Burton, Jack. "The Blue Book of Broadway Musicals." Page 166.

Eells, George. "The Life that Late He Led: A Biography of Cole Porter" 1967. G. P. Putnam's Sons; Original from the University of Michigan. Page 331.

Ewen, David. "American Songwriters: An H. W. Wilson Biographical Dictionary." Page 294.

Francis, Daniel. "The Imaginary Indian: the image of the Indian in Canadian culture. 1992. Page 241.

Jessup, Lynda. "Antimodernism and Artistic Experience: policing the boundaries of Modernity" University of Toronto Press 2001. Pages vii, 36, 37, 38, 39, 47 photos 2.7, 2.8.

Kronenberger, Louis. "The Best Plays." 1969 Dodd, Mead, [etc.]. Page 467.

Kronenberger, Louis. "The Best Plays." 1989. Dodd, Mead, [etc.]. Original from the University of Michigan. Page 495.

Mannik, Lynda. "Canadian Indian Cowboys in Australia: Representation, Rodeo, and the RCMP at the Royal Easter.Show 1939." 2006. Page 182.

Mantle, Burns; Guernsey, Otis L.; Chapman, John Arthur; Sherwood, Garrison P.; Kronenberger, Louis. "The Best Plays." 1920. Dodd, Mead, [etc.].; Original from Stanford University. Page 467.

Mantle, Burns. "The Best Plays of 1919 to 1920 and the Year Book of the Drama in America." 2005. Kessinger Publishing. Page 366.

Mariani, Paul J. "William Carlos Williams: A New World Naked." 1990. W. W. Norton & Company. Page 182.

New York State Historical Association. "Proceedings of the New York State Historical Association: Annual Meeting with Constitution. 1919. New York State Historical Association. Page 113.

New York State Historical Association. "Quarterly Journal of the New York State Historical Association, The." 1931. New York State Historical Association; Original from Stanford University. Page 113.

Norton, Richard C. "A Chronology of American Musical Theater."

Phillips, Ruth B. and Steiner, Christopher Burghard. "Unpacking Culture: art and commodity in colonial and postcolonial worlds." 1999. University of California Press. Pages 305, 306, and 377.

Radforth, Ian. "Royal Spectacle: The 1860 Visit Of The Prince Of Wales To Canada And The United States." 2004. Page 421.

Schochet, Gordon J. and Phillips, Mark. "Questions of Tradition." 2004. University of Toronto Press. Page 64.

Thayer, Scofield and Moore, Marianne, editors. "The Dial." 1918. Page 728.

Exhibit

Daily Gazette. New York. Thursday, May 21, 2009. "Native Talent on View." Iroquois Indian Museum, Howes Cave, New York. www.dailygazett.com

Messina Observer. New York. Tuesday, March 16, 1980. "St. Regis Senior Citizens Find Their Roots at Cultural Center." Kanien'kehaka Raotitiohkwa Cultural Center, Kahnawake.

New York Times, The. New York. January 11, 2002. Glueck, Grace. "Design Review: How Iroquois Artists Turned Trespassers into Tourists." Atada (AntiqueTribal Art Dealers Association, Inc.) 2002.

WPBS TV. A Year of Women Series. http://www.wpbstv.org/YearOfWomen/lesson%20pageDeer.pdf

CHAPTER SIX: LIFE BEYOND THE FOOTLIGHTS
Romance

Boy from Back Home—Correspondence of Sylvia Trudeau. March, 2008.

Race Car Drive—Conversations with Sylvia Trudeau. January 2008.

New York Times. New York. November 19, 1919. "A Real Indian."

Port Arthur News, The. February 9, 1936. "They Love Abe's Love-Songs BUT."

Native American Activism, Patriotism, Civic and Social Activities

Albany Evening Journal. Albany, New York. Tuesday, April 15, 1924. "Affairs in the Social World."

Appleton Post Crescent. Appleton, Wisconsin. August 1, 1925. "Six Nations" to Install 18 Oneida."

Daily Item. Port Chester, New York. August 8, 1932.

Daily Northwest, The. Oshkosh, Wisconsin. March 19, 1921. Malone, Paul R. "On Warpath for Votes for Americans."

Fort Wayne News and Sentinel. Indiana. "Princess White Deer wants votes for squaws. New "Susan B. Anthony."

Frederick Post, The. Frederick, Maryland. Thursday Morning, May 17, 1934. Harrison, Paul. "In New York."

Galveston Daily News, The. Galveston, Texas. June 5, 1927. "An Indian Revue."

Lime Springs Herald, The. Iowa. September 7, 1933. "Who is The Greatest Indian of Today."

Lowell Sun, The. Lowell Massachusetts. Thursday, May 17, 1934. Harrison, Paul. "In New York."

Modesto Evening News. Modesto California. March 19, 1921. Front page. "Votes for Squaw is Battle cry for Mohawk Indians."

New Castle News. January 4, 1918. "Fails to Fool Indian Princess."

New York Times, The. New York. "Indians Present Benefit" February 22, 1932.

New York Times, The. New York. November 9, 1934. "News of the Stage."

Niagara Falls Gazette. New York. May 15, 1934.
Norwood News. St. Lawrence County, NewYork. March 3, 1926.
Oakland Tribune. Oakland California. March 19, 1921.
  Malone, Paul R. "A Indian Maiden is out after Votes."
Old Fulton Post Card. www.fultonhistory.com
  Brooklyn Daily Eagle, The. New York. Monday, September 30, 1929. "Unification to Preserve Identity of Native Race…"
  Brooklyn Daily Eagle, The. New York. October 23, 1929. "Fete to Recall L.I. Battle of 1776 Tomorrow."
  Brooklyn Daily Eagle, The. New York. February, 1932. "Next Sunday Patyatuma."
  Brooklyn Daily Eagle, The. New York. 1932."Unique Celebration."
Potsdam Courier. Potsdam, New York. June 29, 1927 "Indian Princess Visits Former Hogansburg Home."
Poughkeepsie Eagle News. New York. May 23, 1934.
Progress Review. LaPorte City, Iowa. September 7, 1933 "Who is The Greatest Indian of Today."
Scrapbooks and photographs of Princess White Deer, The private collection of Sylvia Trudeau. Courtesy of Sylvia Trudeau.
  The Confederated Indian Tribes of America, invitation 1934.
  Aztec Ball Invitation. February 6, 1925.
  Correspondence: Crown Prince NR Ostgaard to James Deer. May 5, 1939.
Syracuse Herald. New York. February 11, 1928. "Featured Dancer 6 Nations Central NY."
Syracuse Journal. New York. March 19, 1921. "Redskin Lady Boldly Hits Suffrage Trail."
Syracuse Herald. New York. May 15, 1934.
Warren Tribune, The. Warren, Pennsylvania. May 11, 1927.
  Abbott, Amy "Her Day of Work and Play."
Watertown Daily Times. Watertown, NewYork. March 1, 1976. "50 Years Ago."

1937—A Very Good Year
Russet Mantle

Internet Broadway Database, Russet Mantle www.ibdb.com
New York Times, The. New York. 1936. "Chief Accepted for Lead in New Play by Robert Coleman."
"A Handbook of Oklahoma Writers." Excerpted by Mary Hays Marable and Elaine Boyland, University of Oklahoma Press. Norman. 1939. Pages 93–96. Rollie Lynn Riggs—American Playwright http://members.cox.net/lynn.riggs/Lynn Riggs.htm
Time Magzine. New York. Monday, January 27, 1936. "New Play in Manhattan."

Political blunder and the Iroquois Confederacy

Auburn Citizen, The. New York. Friday, February 24, 1922. "Chiefs of Six Nations in Conference in Albany."
Binghampton Press, The. New York. Tuesday Evening, March 2, 1926."The St. Regis Indians want to own Syracuse."
Buffalo Express. Buffalo, New York. Sunday, November 22, 1925. "Buffalo Lawyer one of Staff Fighting Claims of Indians."
Milwaukee Sentinel, The. Wisconsin. July 1, 1937. Peach Section. "Invite From Indians."
Plattsburgh Daily Press. Plattsburgh, New York. Wednesday, July 7, 1937. "Indians Urge a Union for World Peace—Six Nations Iroquois In Conclave Monday at Hogansburg."
Scrapbooks and photographs of Princess White Deer, The private collection of Sylvia Trudeau. Courtesy of Sylvia Trudeau.
Program of The Hodeinonkseonin The League of the Iroquois, July 5, 1937.
Correspondence War Department Washington. June 28, 1937. Mr. James Deer, 126 Beech Street, Yonkers, NY.

Correspondence Canadian Legation. Washington, D.C., June 29, 1937. Mr. James Deer, Honorary Head Chief and Chief of the Mohawks, St. Regis Reservation, 126 Beech Street, Yonkers, NY.

Correspondence The White House, Washington, D.C., July 2, 1937. Mr. James Deer, 126 Beech Street, Yonkers, NY.

Kiwanis Club, Aug 25, 1937.

Wampum Chronicles, The. www.wampumchronicles.com/mohawkschool.html

Indians Bid for Manhattan

Middletown Times Herald. Middletown, New York. November 20, 1937. Indians Bid for Manhattan Island.

Edwardsville Intelligencer. Edwardsville, Illinois. November 20, 1937. Indians Bid for Manhattan Island.

Feather from an Indian Headdress

Kanien'kehaka Raotitiohkwa Cultural Center, Kahnawake.

Personal notes of Esther Deer on her father and King Haakon of Norway. Courtesy of Sylvia Trudeau.

Scrapbooks and photographs of Princess White Deer, The private collection of Sylvia Trudeau. Courtesy of Sylvia Trudeau.

Memorandum of Eric Palmer.

Correspondence Walter L. Main. Andover, Ohio. May 18, 1938. Jas. D. Deer, 126 Beech Street, Yonkers, NY.

Correspondence Gordon W. Lillie, Pawnee Bill. Pawnee Ohio. June 13, 1938.

Pursuit of the Wolf Belt

Fort Covington Sun. Fort Covington, New York. December 24, 1970. Front page.

Hogansburg, Press Republican. New York. December 12, 1970. Page 5. "NY.Fire destroys old hotel." St. Regis, Que.
Watertown Daily Times. New York. December 9, 1970.
Scrapbooks and photographs of Princess White Deer, The private collection of Sylvia Trudeau. Courtesy of Sylvia Trudeau.
    Gillette, Charles E., The University of the State of New York, The State Education Department New York State Museum and Science Service Albany, NY. Correspondence to Sylvia Trudeau, Lachine, Quebec Canada and to Esther Deer, New York, NY. February 5, 1971.

Death Tolls

Massena Observer The. Massena, New York. Thursday, July 2, 1925. "Dollar Day is Great Success."
New York Times, The. New York. July 12, 1939. Obituary of James Deer.
New York Times, The. New York. July 15, 1959. Obituary of Georgette Deer.
Otsego Farmer, The. Cooperstown, New York. Friday, July 14, 1939. "Last Mohawk Chief Passes Away at 73 at Yonker's Hospital."
Potsdam Courier. Potsdam, New York. June 29, 1927. "Indian Princess Visits Former Hogansburg Home."
Port Covington Sun. New York. September 1, 1966. Ester Deer and her cousin, Mrs. Sylvia Trudeau.
Yonkers Statesman. Yonkers, NY. July 11, 1939. "Chief of Mohawks Dies Here at 73."
Yonkers Statesman. Yonkers, New York. April 20, 1940. "The Final Curtain" John Deer.

Living to Be One Hundred

People's Voice, The. Thursday, October 31, 1991. "Princess White Deer Turns 100 Years Old!!"

Scrapbooks and photographs of Princess White Deer, The private collection of Sylvia Trudeau. Courtesy of Sylvia Trudeau.

Correspondence From Longar Ebony Ensemble, Ltd to President George Bush. Oct. 15, 1991.

Exerpt from the letter enclosed with Esther Deer's Last Will and Testament, Courtesy of Sylvia Trudeau.

Photo Credits

Cover Photograph, Curt E. Engelbrecht, from the author's collection.

Pages 22, 35, 46, 48, 93, and 184, courtesy of the Akwesasne Museum.

Pages 28–29, 44, 59, 62, 71, 72, 75, 82, 111, 117, 121, 124, 126, 183, and 189, from the author's collection.

Pages, 134 and 135, courtesy of the Sparta Library.

Pages 142, from the Library of Congress, Prints & Photographs Division, Arnold Genthe Collection.

Page 145, Alfred Cheney Johnston, courtesy of www.alfredcheneyjohnston.com

Page 147 and 152, © 2012 Curatorial Assistance, Inc./E.O. Hoppé Estate Collection.

Page 175, Harris & Ewing, from the Library of Congress, Prints & Photographs Division.

Made in the USA
Middletown, DE
11 December 2020